THE

SALES
PLAYBOOK

PLAYBOOK

**The #1 Sales System to set your people
up for success, scale your business
and delight your customers**

NAOMI OYSTON

DEDICATED TO

Andy and Tiana – who believe in me, see the best in me, and inspire me to SHINE.

FREE 1-1 SALES & SERVICE STRATEGY ASSESSMENT

The purpose of this book is to help you create and document a comprehensive Sales & Service Strategy that will be perfect for your business and generate results that matter most.

We know that creating a powerful Sales & Service Strategy is perhaps the most important and valuable thing you can do for your business, yet it may be overwhelming at times. It just feels like another thing on your never-ending to-do list. You know it makes sense and you want to implement it, and it seems simple enough on paper, but in reality, it may not always feel easy.

We are here to support you with the process by asking the hard questions, engaging your people, keeping you on track, and ensuring your content is industry best practice.

You don't have to do it alone!

Our tailored coaching support programs mean that we are focusing on the highest value areas for your business.

The first step is to understand where you're at right now, where you'd like to be in the future, and then to create an action plan to get you there. It's not a one-size-fits-all approach but rather something where we will both agree on the best possible solution for you.

We do this through a no-obligation and no-cost strategy call. If it makes sense for us to work together after that –

fantastic. If not, we are happy to provide you with clarity around what options are available and you can choose your path from there.

We are here to help, whether that's now, in a few chapters, or at the end of the book. You can schedule your free exploratory call on the link below:

www.shineexecutive.com.au/salesstrategy

IT'S EASY TO GET STARTED

Download your FREE Playbook Template Now!

Before you dive in to discover the concepts within the Sales Playbook – Playbook, make sure to download your template so you're ready to get started straight away.

I'm sure that as you read through each of the focus areas within the book, you will be thinking about what this looks like for you in your business. Almost all the concepts we discuss will be relevant for ANY business, regardless of the size or your market offerings.

To make things as easy and convenient as possible for you to quickly put ideas into action, our Playbook template is created in Word format so you can capture your ideas as you go.

Sometimes seeing the entire system within a working document helps to understand just how simple the journey ahead is if you take it step by step. How do you eat an elephant? One bite at a time.

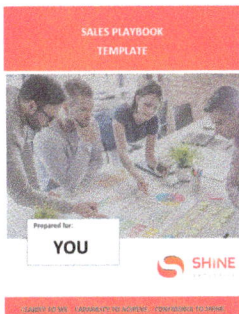

If you'd like to get started with our easy prepared-for-you template, just visit:

www.shineexecutive.com.au/playbooktemplate

Download Now ⬇

ENDORSEMENTS

Sales Playbooks Work!

I was first introduced to the concept of Sales Playbooks working with USA-based Sales and Hyper Growth Systems trainer Jack Daly around 20 years ago. Jack's processes have helped organisations globally to achieve high performance in the areas of sales, leadership, and culture.

One of the key foundations of Jack's program is **working out what works,** capturing best practice, and documenting it into a step-by-step game-winning playbook.

As a result of working with Jack and seeing just how powerful his processes were, I became the Head Coach for Leverage Sales Coaching Australia and New Zealand, where I have taught the Jack Daly Sales Systems to CEOs, Managing Directors, Sales Managers, and Sales teams since. All my clients have created Sales Playbooks and they use them daily to drive results.

It was my pleasure to welcome Naomi Oyston into my coaching team around 10 years ago. I got to see her in action, supporting her clients to thrive using the Jack Daly framework. She has a unique talent of being able to make the complex simple and also possesses a genuine desire to help others succeed.

Naomi and I have continued to work together for many years creating numerous Sales Playbooks for clients and she has distilled this knowledge into a very comprehensive how-to guide in this book – beginning with the Jack Daly principles and then expanding into so many other aspects that are relevant for today's organisations.

I can honestly say that Sales Playbooks work! I've seen them in action for so long now that it is a no-brainer. When we stop "winging it" and approach the Sales & Service journey in a way that is strategic, methodical, and purposeful, results will follow.

This book will show you the pathway to achieving extraordinary results, and if you're looking for someone to guide you along the journey of creating your own Sales Playbook, Naomi is the absolute expert.

Serge Romano, Head Coach Australia & NZ

A Template for Growth and Best Practice

Having worked in B2B sales and marketing environments for the last 15 years, I've seen the value of highly motivated and resourced sales teams: a deep level of understanding of their customers' business priorities and the ability to create long-lasting relationships.

Repeat business and recommendations as a sales strategy is based on trust and communication. If sales and marketing teams can achieve this through effective training and tools, then everyone is a winner!

I've had the absolute fortune to work with Naomi and harness her expertise with my team. Her engaging style, enthusiasm, and proven methodology are highly effective. Her ability to bring people along on the sales excellence journey and provide realistic and actionable strategies have increased the effectiveness of my team and provided a template for growth and best practice.

I highly recommend this resource for anyone looking to upskill their team and template their sales strategy and behaviours.

Sascha Sinclair, Head of Sales and Marketing

Packed Full of High-Impact Strategies and Tools

Naomi has been part of the growth and success of Fallon Solutions for at least half a dozen years now.

Helping us initially with building Sales & Service Playbooks, completing a market scan of software competitors, conducting our annual staff survey, and helping us to use that knowledge to improve our culture, Naomi has a broad range of skills that can help you grow into a world-class organisation. Her passion for customer service and business improvement is at 150% every single day she works with you.

Her easy-to-read book is packed full of high-impact strategies and tools. Implement and embed the concepts now in your organisation, and you will see a massive improvement.

Or if you're struggling to find time in your daily whirlwind, give Naomi a call.

Mark Denning, Owner and Managing Director

Successful Business Template

I've been in the Accounting and Financial Planning industry for a long time now and have not come across a better way to implement a Sales & Service strategy. When I was looking to review our business practices 10 years ago, I asked Naomi Oyston to introduce me to her framework to build an ideal customer base. By documenting our policies and procedures, we now have a successful business template to easily manage our sales processes.

Better still, by engaging with our ideal customers for our accounting practice, our repeat business has also increased because we're hitting our service targets more effectively. This has resulted in receiving a high level of referrals from our **Raving Fans**.

In fact, we have also been using the very principles Naomi is introducing with her new book *The Sales Playbook* in our business consulting practice. I am so glad that Naomi has decided to publish her extensive knowledge on this topic and have no doubt it will help many entrepreneurs and small business owners become more successful.

Robert Bauman, Accountant and Financial Planner

Nothing is as Important as Revenue

There are many things that we need to get right to run a successful business, but NOTHING is as important as generating consistent revenue. When we get this right, everything else becomes so much easier.

We engaged Naomi to help us develop our Sales Playbook and she was a tremendous support in documenting our processes. While we have a great deal of industry capability from years of experience, it is challenging to capture all of this succinctly on your own as quite frankly, you're just not sure where to start. Naomi's Playbook system provided us with a clear structure that allowed us to unpack everything we knew and put it into a document that our team members could understand and implement.

I have no hesitation in recommending Naomi to any business leader who understands the power of a robust revenue creation strategy and the value of a well-documented process.

Rachel Trihey, CEO

In the Driver's Seat for Success

My friend and business leader Naomi is a master at inspiring, coaching, and leading people to success. I have known and worked with Naomi since 2005, initially as a client for my own training and then also referring many other people, all of whom have gone from strength to strength with personal and professional success. She is a genius who loves to share her knowledge and experience in an easy-to-understand and useful way.

I lead large IT&T companies for sales and customer outcomes. Naomi's coaching over these years has allowed me to understand the core success of any business is how you refine and embed your best practices.

If you are truly ready to grow your career, sales team, and business, this book will definitely put you right in the driver's seat for success.

Right now, you are holding a book in your hands that will change the way you interact with people and lead. This book provides a detailed structure that will allow people starting out to become an inspirational sales leader or a refresher for someone who is looking for the accelerate their business and/or career.

I highly recommend this book, and I am very excited to be a part of this journey.

Graham O'Davis, General Manager

PREFACE

How to know if this book is for you

On the outside, people look at you and think, "This person has got it all together." You've achieved a level of success out of blood, sweat, and tears – doing the work to get where you are and delivering results that matter by learning along the way over the years. You know what works, your clients like you, you're good at what you do, and now you're ready for the next level.

But you realise that your own individual success can only take you so far. It is no longer about how good you are but instead how good your people can become. You see massive growth opportunities in the market, but to achieve this you need to create and maintain a high performing sales team who will consistently deliver the type of service excellence that sets you up as a market leader. You have big plans with big targets that will not be achieved without a results focused strategic approach to the sales process.

You also know that sales are the foundation of your business success – without sales, you have no business!

Getting your sales strategy right creates the revenue to support all other functions within your business. It is the lifeblood that allows everything else to thrive and expand: without strong sales, your business will wither and retract. You know it is too important to be left to chance and quietly hoping that it will work itself out on its own.

You wish that you could just hire people who "get it", but it's not always that easy. Onboarding, training, and developing your sales team is time-consuming and cumbersome. Asking your highest performers to train the new starters slows them down and distracts them from doing what they need to do. But you also want your people to share best practice and get up to speed quickly with a consistent, customer-centred approach.

Unfortunately, you also know that when important knowledge is shared by word of mouth, sometimes key messages get distorted through "Chinese whispers". You know there needs to be a source of truth that is documented so everyone is singing from the same hymn sheet. You know that without a clear process that outlines the defined expectations, your people are "winging it" – even with the best intentions – and, therefore, your customer experience and results will be impacted accordingly.

You seem to spend most of your time trying to get your low performers up to speed or putting out bushfires when customers get upset or mistakes are made.

At times, leading a sales team feels a bit like herding cats trying to get everyone on the same page – you just want to get all your ducks in a row so you can move forward.

Herding Cats vs. Ducks in a Row

"A futile attempt to control that which is inherently uncontrollable"

"To be well prepared, organised and ready for whats about to happen"

You know your business can make a bigger impact.

You know you have so much more that you can achieve.

You know that you're ready to get scale and efficiency as the foundation of revenue, retention, growth, and sales targets.

You see that the collective brains trust is stronger than any individual, and exponential momentum can be created from a united team who take ownership to help each other succeed.

You want to deliver first-class service to your customers because you know how much it hurts your bottom line when your good customers leave and you have to find new ones to replace them. You also know the power of having **Raving Fans** as customers who open doors and refer valuable business opportunities to you.

You want to create a proactive, empowering sales culture that helps your team to generate LEVERAGE – better results with less effort by adopting best practice alongside high-value systems and processes.

You are ready to fast track to a higher level of performance, but you haven't been sure where to start...

Until now.

You're in the right place at the right time right now!

Strap yourself in and we will work through the step-by-step process to creating a Sales Playbook that is perfect for your unique business needs and goals.

"Find the heart of it, make the complex simple, and you can achieve mastery. With mastery what was once hard becomes easy."

– Dan Millman

THE LEGEND OF THE HAPPY, LAZY, AND LUCKY SALESPERSON

It may seem paradoxical, but in my experience, some of the most successful salespeople are not necessarily the ones who work the hardest.

In the early stages of my career, I worked with a man called Peter. He was a charming, charismatic kind of person who was friendly and well-liked within the business. He had a beautiful wife, happy high-achieving kids, and a healthy lifestyle surrounded by great friends and family. Not only did he have his personal life in order, but he was also consistently in the top three national high achievers in the business for both sales and customer satisfaction. He worked on the largest accounts and would regularly write deals that were five to ten times the value of the average operator.

Better still, he didn't even seem to work that hard! Because he was so good at looking after his customers, he received

a high level of personal referrals to key prospects – business seemed to just fall out of the sky and into his lap. He only handled the high-value tasks that required his personal attention while handing everything else off to others (with developing salespeople like me feeling grateful for the smaller deals he gave them).

Each Friday he would clock off at midday to take clients or introducers out to lunch, earning the nickname of *Sir Lunchalot*. Little did we realise at the time that his weekly targets were usually achieved by Wednesday afternoon due to his focused actions earlier in the week – this was just as the rest of us were still scrambling Friday afternoon to get everything through!

Then, one day, he won a fabulous new car in a raffle from a ticket that he'd bought at a client's fundraising event for charity. As he had a fully maintained company vehicle, he promptly sold the car and used the money as a deposit on an investment property.

Jeez! This guy was the happiest, laziest, and luckiest person ever...

Or was he?

Considering the Pareto principle, it is of course expected and common to see that the top 20% of salespeople write 80% of the group's results. They do this not by working more hours, but by being more deliberate, strategic, and focused – **doing the right activities, in the right ways, consistently** – to create valued outcomes with more ease and less effort. They seem to do less work than other team members and are also happier in themselves and their role.

What's really happening is they don't get caught up in the minutiae, drama, or stories about why things can't work because they're busy just getting on with things with a can-do attitude. They achieve results that they're proud of, love what they do, and have plenty of energy left to enjoy their life outside of work as well.

On the outside, it looks like they're just lucky. Everything they touch seems to turn to gold. The truth is, they're working smarter, not harder. They have developed the mindset, habits, time management, and disciplines that create mastery. Success comes easy to them because of the work they've done to set themselves up first through training, practice, coaching, and feedback.

The trick, then, to being lucky, lazy, happy, and successful is to master the high-leverage activities and do them better than anyone else.

The harder we work at mastering the process, the luckier we get with results, and the easier everything becomes.

"Luck is what happens when preparation meets opportunity." Seneca

And this... is the ultimate competitive advantage.

Successful sales habits can be taught.

Mastery can be achieved through focused and consistent discipline.

Your Sales Playbook is the first step.

TABLE OF CONTENTS

If you can't describe what you are doing as a process, you don't know what you're doing."

– Edward Deming

INTRODUCTION

What is a Sales Playbook?

The purpose of a Sales Playbook is to capture best practice, street proven sales processes, and insights that creates consistent high performance through working SMARTER not HARDER. A well-designed, relevant, and engaging playbook will create more high performers *more quickly* and help close the gap for developing team members by building confidence, clarity, and capability.

Your Sales Playbook is the bridge between a go-to-market strategy (GTM) and Tactical Execution. It is a set of clearly defined steps and methods of communication between your business and your prospects or customers. Whether you are a business startup, an established SME, or a large corporation, the principles of Sales & Service Excellence remain the same.

There is no one-size-fits-all sales strategy; however, there is a best practice approach to defining what will work for your organisation and capturing this in a way that others can understand and learn from.

Your playbook begins with a standard template which is then tailored to your unique business needs, goals, and market opportunities in consultation with your key people. This may also be supported by an external consultant who can guide you through the process to help unpack the knowledge within your organisation.

The power of your Sales Playbook is in the tailoring of the content specifically for your organisation. The best playbooks are seen as a go-to guide and are never complete because they are continually evolving when fresh insights arise over time.

A well-crafted Sales Playbook sets the benchmarks and expectations that create your organisational customer fulfilment DNA: who you are, what you do, and how you do it better than anyone else. It helps your people to understand the **WHY, WHAT, WHEN,** and **HOW** to do the activities that will drive successful outcomes.

A sales-based organisation without a process cannot scale predictably. Your process needs to be as simple as possible but robust enough that all employees can plug in to generate predictable results.

Most importantly, success in any business relies on a team of people who work together, embracing clearly defined high-value activities with a common purpose of delivering a seamless, quality customer experience – remembering that without customers there is no business. Everyone needs to be on the same page, understanding how their role contributes to creating **Raving Fans** who ultimately become your best advocates and strongest sales strategy.

Simply put, the path outlined within your playbook will show HOW to be successful in:

- Differentiating yourselves from your competitors
- Demonstrating value and delivering service excellence to your ideal customers
- Winning more of the right deals
- Increasing revenue, repeat business, and retention
- Generating quality referrals and testimonials
- Creating reliability and predictability of future results
- Onboarding and coaching individuals for high performance
- Delivering consistently good customer experiences
- Staying true to your core values, brand, and what is most important to your organisation

A Sales Playbook is...	A Sales Playbook is not...
√ Easy to understand and implement	x Complex policies and procedures
√ For everyone in the business	x Just for salespeople
√ A work in progress – a living document with continual improvement	x Completed once – then set and forget
√ Teaching people how to fish	x Giving them a fish

√ Customer-centred with service excellence a key part of the sales process	x Limited to the initial sales process alone
√ Your team's collective "brain" as a single source of knowledge	x Created in the ivory tower and handed down
√ Aimed at revenue generation and customer fulfilment activities	x Bogged down with operational issues
√ Successful from action: defining, training, embedding, and improving high-value activities and practices	x A quick fix by simply reading the material – to know and to not do is to not know
√ Tailored to your unique business needs, strengths, and opportunities	x An off-the-shelf generic solution
√ Single source of knowledge and practices	x Everyone winging it with their own "style"
√ Used for recruitment, onboarding, and coaching on an ongoing basis	x Just an initial training tool
√ Empowering happy, successful employees who take ownership of the process because they see the value	x Forcing people to do something they don't want or need to do
√ Consistency of messaging throughout the business	x "Chinese Whispers" from individual interpretations

√ Combines mindset, skill set, and toolkit to succeed with authenticity and integrity	x A training manual based on process alone

Do we need a Sales Playbook? Is now the right time?

If you're like most business leaders, improving your current results or setting yourself up for success in achieving future growth goals is always a priority.

Is now the right time to invest in creating a Sales Playbook? Why not answer the 10-question quiz below to gain clarity.

Statement	Agree	Unsure	Disagree
1. All salespeople are consistently achieving their targets.			
2. Our customers are highly satisfied and regularly provide quality referrals.			
3. We have as many quality leads as we need to achieve our goals.			
4. Our salespeople know our point of difference in the market and how to win against our major competitors.			
5. Our pipeline management provides accurate forecasting of results.			

6. We can quickly bring new sales recruits up to speed to achieve their targets within their first 90 days.			
7. Salespeople can share relevant success stories and case studies with prospects to build trust and confidence.			
8. Our team are consistently generating new quality opportunities through multiple centres of influence.			
9. We have captured best practice processes from our high performers to ensure we are not missing valuable opportunities.			
10. Our salespeople know how to ask powerful discovery questions in various situations to uncover pain points and opportunities; they are also able to confidently handle resistance or objections.			

Your answers to the above questions will tell you a story about where you're at right now and the answer will be obvious. If you've answered "Agree" to everything, congratulations – you have a very strong foundation. If not, perhaps there is some work to be done...

"If you believe you are right, or believe you are wrong you're right. Whenever you are certain about something you will support it. As we develop new beliefs, our behaviour will change to support this."

– Tony Robbins

Useful Presuppositions About Creating Your Sales Playbook

Before you get started, it is important to begin with core beliefs around how we view the world of sales. Ultimately, our beliefs create our results, so it makes sense to begin with the end in mind and choose the beliefs that will support our success.

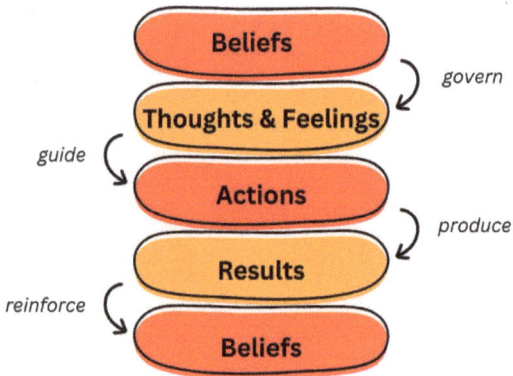

Here are some of my core beliefs that have formed a useful foundation for everything that I do. You may wish to create or add some of your own to this list.

1. Without sales, there is no business. Sales is the lifeblood of every business as it generates the revenue required for everything else to flourish. It is the single most important function of every business.

2. Sales is not a dirty word – it is how we help our customers find valued solutions. When I approach sales with a desire to help rather than sell, everything flows.

3. Sales is simply an exchange of value – if we can create more value than the cost in the customer's eyes, sales is easy. If not, sales will always be hard.

4. Sales is the highest form of service. It's about understanding needs, opportunities, desires, or challenges while delivering a quality solution better than anyone else.

5. We are all in sales – any time we are exchanging value through goods and services for revenue, we are in the sales game. Sales has been around since time immemorial. If we want to receive higher rewards, we need to deliver higher value for our customers.

6. Sales is not a department; it is an attitude. Every person within the business should support the sales process regardless of their role. If you're not serving a customer, you're serving someone who is serving a customer. Without customers, there is no business.

7. The purpose of the sales process is to create highly satisfied customers who become **Raving Fans**. This is the true competitive advantage that will deliver exponential returns when leveraged correctly.

8. People like to do business with and refer others to someone they know, like, and trust. No matter what business we are in, we are all in the people business. Interpersonal skills and relationships matter.

9. There are no natural-born salespeople. Sales is a skill set that can be learned and developed by anyone willing to try. Professional sales people are passionate about what they do and act with honesty, integrity, and expertise, all the while taking personal responsibility for their actions and results.

10. The clearer we are about what we are looking for, the easier it is to find it. There are always plenty of customers who we can help. Clarity, resourcefulness, and taking action are keys to success.

"Your customers are only satisfied because their expectations are so low and because no one else is doing better. Just having satisfied customers is not enough anymore. If you really want a booming business, you must create Raving Fans."

– Ken Blanchard

Raving Fans – Your Competitive Advantage and the Ultimate Goal of Your Playbook

The purpose of every business is to create and keep a customer. Customers are the foundation of a business; they keep it in existence and provide the revenue necessary for employment, assets, and operating expenses. Without sales, you have no customers, and without customers, you have no business!

It is not enough to just focus on finding new customers: a dual focus of service excellence needs to be in place. Acquiring new customers can cost up to seven times more than retaining or growing existing customers, yet many businesses see sales as acquisition alone and do not combine their sales strategy with a robust customer service excellence approach. This results in high levels of churn, reputational damage, unnecessary expenses, margin pressure, and stress on everyone involved. You just feel like you're chasing your tail because the runoff is happening faster than you can onboard new business.

The only way to truly create a sustainable, efficient and enjoyable sales environment is to focus on creating **Raving Fans**.

Raving Fans aren't just customers; they are highly engaged with your business and can't help but tell others about your products or services with genuine enthusiasm and excitement. Their referrals carry a high level of implied trust due to their personal experience and will set you up as the preferred provider from the outset.

It makes good business sense to master this process as it will:

- Increase the lifetime value of your customer

- Provide a true differentiator from competitors

Referrals from Raving Fans...

16%
higher lifetime value

30%
higher conversion rate

37%
higher retention rate

4
times more likely to refer others

- Increase the number of qualified referrals

- Reduce the acquisition cost for new customers

- Reduce churn or runoff, therefore increasing retention

- Reduce price sensitivity

- Increase the ease of doing business

- Reduce costs of doing business and increase profitability

- Provide testimonials and case studies

- Give you feedback that helps you improve

- Create new **Raving Fans** who will exponentially grow your business for you...

Simply put, Raving Fans are the easiest, fastest, and most profitable and enjoyable path to success.

From a sales process perspective, it is important to place the customer at the centre of your Sales Playbook. You can then create your content with a view to defining what your customers most want from you and how you can deliver this to them better than anyone else.

"While every business is different, the principles of Sales & Service Excellence are the same – Understand your customer's needs and deliver valued solutions better than anyone else."

– Naomi Oyston

Why your Sales Playbook Can Become your Most Valuable Business Asset

The best Sales Playbooks are the lifeblood of your business. When approached with a comprehensive process, leadership empowerment, and high engagement from team members, the flow on benefits are exponential.

A well compiled Sales Playbook will help you to:

- Provide a clear guide HOW to be successful in sales

- Engage your whole team in owning the process and sharing ideas for continual improvement

- Align all team members with your strategy and their role in your success

- Set expectations around the high payoff activities required – in quantity and quality

- Capture and share "unconscious competence" from high performing individuals

- Enhance consistency, reliability, and predictability of future results

- Identify system weaknesses, gaps, or sales leakage that result in lost opportunities

- Prepare for potential obstacles and be ready to overcome them

- Increase your sales revenue by working smarter, not harder

- Create multiple Raving Fans through excellence in customer service

- Establish a DNA for your organisational sales culture – who you are, what you do, and how you do it

To be successful in creating a robust sales culture, you need to build clarity, capability, and confidence in your people. Your playbook will go a long way towards this and will act as a source of truth for coaching, training, and development purposes.

What are the challenges? How do you overcome them?

The truth is that any business can (and should) have a Sales Playbook; however, while this is a simple concept to understand, putting it into practice is not always easy.

Problem	Solution
x Urgency: While this is a very IMPORTANT piece of work, it is not always the most URGENT and can be pushed to the bottom of the to-do list which can diminish focus.	√ Define this as a high-value non-negotiable priority activity with deadlines in place for each stage.

x Unconscious competence: Much of the information that needs to be completed in the playbook is not conscious. Your best people may struggle to articulate what and how they do what they do. They just do it and think everyone should get it (which they don't).	√ A beginner's mindset is required to unpack the knowledge and break it down into steps. Sometimes this takes someone outside of the business or outside of the role to ask powerful questions.
x Overwhelm: At first, the project can seem a little overwhelming – you know it makes sense but you don't know where to start.	√ Create a project plan with shared responsibilities and regular scheduled check points. Chunk it down into manageable steps.
x Engagement: Team members see it as "someone else's job" and don't take ownership or contribute.	√ Sell the WHY. How is this going to make their roles easier? How will this help them to be more successful by working smarter not harder? Why is their expertise and contribution highly valued and required?
x Differences in opinions: There can often be different ways of approaching situations in sales which can stall momentum. Sometimes this comes from conflicting objectives.	√ The best time to discuss this is BEFORE you're sitting in front of a customer. Best practice clarity needs to be reached through engaging all participants to focus on WHAT rather

	than WHO is right in order to drive results.
x Spending too much time on the aesthetics of the playbook: While appearance and readability is required, the purpose of the playbook is to capture continual improvement through a live and evolving process.	√ Create a dynamic platform that can be quickly and easily updated as required (eg intranet or share point). Functionality is generally more powerful than a PowerPoint or Word document that is difficult to update.
x Perfection not progress: Work will expand to the time allowed – there will always be more work to do. The first objective is to get it done and road test it in practice to see what updates are required.	√ Agree on continuous improvement – progress is better than perfection and done is better than perfect. It is a work-in-progress that should never actually be finished as it will be always evolving on the feedback of users.

"To achieve great things, three things are needed: a strong WHY, a plan, and not quite enough time."

– Naomi Oyston

Preparing to Create your Sales Playbook

Spectacular achievement is always preceded by unspectacular preparation. The best place to start is at the beginning, and the best time to start is when you're too busy because you're more likely to prioritise, delegate, and be motivated by completion.

The following steps will help you to develop a plan that will maximise your impact and engagement within the time and resources you have available.

i) Start with your WHY, then WHAT, then HOW

Your WHY will provide the inspiration necessary for the success of your Sales Playbook. Any organization can explain *what* it does; some can explain *how* they do it; but very few can clearly articulate *why*. WHY is not just money or profit – those are always results.

WHY does your organisation exist?

WHY does it do the things it does?

WHY do customers choose you over your competitors?

WHY do you want to define the Sales Process?

WHY do you care about this?

Begin with clarity around HOW an amazing Sales Playbook for your business will impact:

- Employee experience
- Customer experience
- Market competitive advantage
- Ease of doing business
- Recruitment and onboarding
- Results and profitability

- GROWTH plans and alignment with strategic priorities

- Organisational culture and teamwork

Then consider what these results could look like if you DON'T do this and contrast the outcomes. This will create your purpose and value proposition.

ii) Identify a sponsor, key stakeholders, and WIIFM (What's in it for me)

Starting from the top-down, consider who needs to be involved in this project and how it will benefit them or align with their strategic priorities. Demonstrate how this will add value before you ask for a commitment of their time or resources. Gain the endorsement of a senior leader as a sponsor who can help drive access or urgency if required.

Consider what level of consultation or contribution is appropriate from each area, keeping in mind that the purpose of the Sales Playbook is to bring business units or teams together so collaboration is a key part of the process.

iii) Define your Minimum Viable Product – the Right Amount of Content to Begin

The paradox is that too much process kills sales teams but sales teams will die without process and an understanding of how to win. It is a fine balance between simplicity and complexity, but a good rule of thumb is to determine whether a new team member would be able to understand the content without prior knowledge.

The Sales Playbook template provides you with the suggested content for each area; however, this is obviously subjective and you should establish what will work for you. A great Sales Playbook will continue to grow and evolve over the years, so it does not have to be perfect in the first edition. It can simply begin as your Minimum Viable Product (MVP). Once a small group of users has validated

Amount & Impact of Sales Process

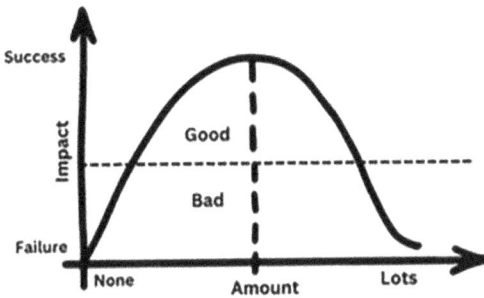

the playbook, you can continue to add content as and when gaps are identified.

iv) Assets and Collateral Register

Your playbook will be successful if it directly aligns with the strategic goals of your business as well as the familiar or known processes in place. This means that it makes sense to team members and creates the bigger picture. There is generally lots of great information held within the business around the sales and customer fulfilment process, but often it is not all in one place.

You should consider what collateral will support your Sales Playbook, where these documents should be held (eg intranet, shared drive) and how you will manage version control. A thorough information gathering plan will result in a strong first version of your playbook; however, it is useful to reference many of these rather than include them. This can reduce the complexity of the playbook and means the focus remains on the most important content for revenue producing.

Some examples of sales collateral are:

- Annual reports
- Sales presentations, pitch decks

- Organisation chart

- Competitor intelligence – how can we win?

- CRM guidelines

- Pipeline management

- Customer satisfaction survey data

- Pricing authorities

- Product or service features, benefits, value propositions, pain points

- Case studies and success stories

- Trade show schedule: set up and processes

- Customer conversation – needs analysis documents

- White papers, ebooks, videos, marketing collateral, style guides

- Qualifying and discovery questions

- Account management – customer segmentation and contact requirements

- Credit authorities

- Common objections and responses

- Customer avatars or personas with target market, pain points, and needs for products and services

- Scripting for gaining appointments and outbound calling

It is good practice to begin with a comprehensive list to track the assets needed so that you have plenty of time to gather your requirements and don't have to do multiple requests. It could also be useful to link the WIIFM benefit and big picture WHY into your requests to gain support from relevant parties.

An example of a table to track this is below.

Contact person	Asset	Request date	Received
Bill – Marketing	White papers Case studies Style guide	March 15	April 1
Jane – EA to GM	Organisation chart Our story Director profiles	March 15	

v) Timeline, checkpoints, and project management

As with any project, an agile approach to managing the completion is required. Depending on your work preferences, some project management software options will be useful, such as:

- Asana

- Trello

- Monday

- Workzone

Some examples of the items that should be included in the project management process are:

- Stakeholder engagement meetings

- Information gathering

- Sales team brainstorming sessions

- Individual responsibilities

- Tracking of assets

- Review and feedback

- Training of key staff

- Implementation rollout

- Review and continuous improvement

It is beneficial for one person to be the "owner" of the playbook and hold the ultimate responsibility for completion, with support from the Executive Sponsor.

"*Everything should be as simple as possible, but not simpler.*"

– Albert Einstein

Introduction: In summary

1. A Sales Playbook is a structured way to capture your end-to-end Sales & Service Strategy in a way that your people can understand, learn from, adopt, take ownership of, and improve over time.

2. Powerful and effective Sales Playbooks are built on the foundation of best practices and then tailored to your unique business needs.

3. Your Sales Playbook can quickly become one of the most valuable revenue-producing assets within your business as it is the HOW to succeed.

4. Creating your own powerful Sales Playbook is simple, but not always easy, so it needs a focused approach and project plan.

5. While your playbook shows the way for best practice activities, you also need to consider how to create resourceful mindsets within your people as it is our beliefs that drive our behaviour and create our results. A toolkit without the mindset will not be enough to succeed.

6. Not only will your people become more successful through applying the concepts within the playbook, your customers will love it too because the process

places customer satisfaction at the centre of everything you do.

7. The ultimate goal of your playbook should be to create **Raving Fans** who will grow your business in a way that:

o Feels joyful and easy – your customers are a pleasure to do work with, they want to do business with you, and they are on board from the onset

o Is profitable – they are less price-sensitive (up to 16% tolerance on pricing due to their innate desire to do business with YOU)

o Is faster – given the level of trust in place, lead times are lower

o Are pre-qualified and know what it is you need to do business

o Multiplies – **Raving Fans** create more **Raving Fans**

o Helps your people to love what they do because of the level of relationships in place

o Becomes your ULTIMATE COMPETITIVE ADVANTAGE

1:

FOUNDATIONS

"*Great stories happen to those who can tell them.*"

– Ira Glass

ORGANISATIONAL OVERVIEW – WHO WE ARE & WHAT WE DO

What is it?

An organisational overview is a summary of a company's history, leadership structure, product or service offerings, priorities, values, and point of difference in the marketplace. The purpose of this is to build a foundation of knowledge and connection to your business.

Why does it matter?

Our goal is for our people to become evangelists: passionate advocates who spread the word about our business, inspiring others to become customers, supporters, or referrers. A business evangelist will use positive word-of-mouth messages through stories that connect people with your purpose, products, and history.

This begins with a deep understanding and emotional connection to the WHO, WHY, HOW, WHEN, and WHAT of your business.

Every successful business has a story. While your background is essential to understand, where you're going in the future is more important. Make sure this is inspiring and aspirational to ensure that your team can buy into your vision. This is your opportunity to capture the essence of your business in a way that facilitates knowledge, pride, passion, and connection.

Exercise: Keys to your organisational overview

**Take action
Complete this** ☝

- Welcome from the directors

- Background

- Why we are successful – what makes us good at what we do

- Directors and leadership team (make it fun and interesting)

- Future vision

- Organisation chart

- What is most important to us:

  √ Vision
  √ Purpose
  √ Values
  √ Mission
  √ Our WHY

- What are we passionate about?

- Strategic priorities

"Great sales cultures attract, retain, motivate, and grow talented employees.
To win the marketplace, you must first win the workplace."

– Naomi Oyston

OUR SALES CULTURE

What is it?

Your Sales Culture can be loosely described as "how we do things around here". It is the collective definition of beliefs, attitudes, behaviours, disciplines, and actions of the employees within your organisation. While it can sometimes be hard to put into words, your Sales Culture is how it feels to work in your business environment.

A clearly defined Sales Culture will allow you to attract and connect with the right type of people who will thrive within your environment. If you do not deliberately or strategically create your sales culture, your people will do it for you – and it may not be what you would choose.

Why does it matter?

A positive workplace environment will enhance employee wellbeing, productivity, performance, customer interaction, collaboration and teamwork, trust, transparency, retention, and recruitment of new employees.

A negative workplace environment can create employee churn, fear of recrimination, stress, unhealthy conflict, inconsistent results, and reputational damage.

When people understand the type of Sales Culture that you are intentionally creating, things make more sense. This means they are clear about your expectations on "how we do things around here" in a way that is good for business, good for team members, and good for customers.

Exercise: What defines our Sales Culture

**Take action
Complete this**

Pick your top 10 – or come up with your own – priorities for your Sales Culture and expand on what good looks like for you.

- Attitudes
- Behaviours
- Skills
- Experience
- Growth strategy/ mindset
- Continual improvement
- Willingness to learn
- Coaching for success
- Hunter v Farmer v Fisherman sales
- Trade shows and events

- Competitive
- Integrity
- Relationship-based
- Work quality
- Social
- Industry knowledge
- Profitable business
- Repeat business
- Referrals
- Networks
- Collaboration
- Celebrating success

- Demonstrated value to clients
- Accountability
- Trust
- Service excellence
- Goals
- Teamwork
- Feedback
- High-value activities
- Staying in touch
- Modelling best practice
- Recognition and reward

- Caring for each other
- Work-life balance
- Fun and happiness

- Sharing knowledge
- Taking action
- Done is better than perfect

- Mistakes help us to learn

"*You can't manage what you don't measure.*"

– Peter F Drucker

SALES METRICS

What is it?

Sales metrics are data points that gauge sales performance or activity levels on an individual, team, or organisational level. The metrics help track progress towards goals, forecast results, prepare for future needs, identify best practices, benchmark performance, and also discover potential issues sooner rather than later.

There are many different metrics that organisations may use as performance indicators; however, trying to focus on too many can be counter-productive, so it makes good business sense to choose the ones that will have the greatest impact if you get them right – or create the most damage if you get them wrong.

Some examples are:

- Revenue

  √ Gross sales
  √ Revenue by product or service
  √ Margins by product or service
  √ New business
  √ Repeat business
  √ Trends – month on month, year on year
  √ Profit after expenses

- Individual or team performance

√ Actual v target results

√ Activity levels

√ Conversion rates

√ Weighted pipeline value

√ Revenue and margin performance

√ Deals lost

√ Length of sales cycle

- Customers

√ Net Promoter Score (NPS) – customer loyalty and satisfaction

√ Referrals provided

√ Product penetration

√ Average customer lifetime value

√ Business held with other providers

√ Market penetration

√ Customer acquisition costs

Why does it matter?

Energy flows where focus goes – that's why it's important to take the guesswork out of your success and get the real data so you can make informed decisions about what's working well and what could be better.

You can't manage what you don't measure and the numbers don't lie: they'll tell you a story that could very well act as the canary in the coalmine to alert you to potential dangers in your business before it is too late. It also allows you to identify your wins and to deep dive in order to understand what's working well and how to amplify your team's focus in these areas by sharing best practices.

Every business should have short- and long-term metrics that provide real-time measures on a daily, weekly, monthly, quarterly, or annual basis. Ideally you should choose your top five focus areas and build a Results Dashboard to always have the numbers at your fingertips. These numbers can then be discussed in your team meetings, one-to-ones, coaching conversations, or leadership meetings.

If you don't know where you're going, any road will get you there, so smart sales metrics with clear expectations are needed to set your people up for success.

Exercise: Sales metrics that measure our success

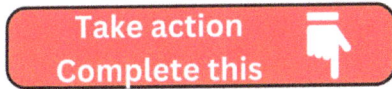

Take action
Complete this

Explain what measures are most important in your business. How do you measure success? Use the examples above or feel free to come up with your own.

"Make everything about the success of your sales team so they can focus on the success of your customers."

– Tony Hughes

SALES ENABLEMENT AND MARKETING STRATEGY

What is it?

Sales enablement is the ecosystem that supports customer-facing employees to engage with various stakeholders and customers, where all departments within the business have a sales-centric mindset. Sales enablement is supported through marketing activities including branding, promotion, events, customer communications, and lead generation.

Why does it matter?

The goal of sales enablement is to create a sales process that is as simple as possible but robust enough that every team member can understand their role and expectations so that we can create scale, efficiency, and predictability of results. It is finding the balance between structure and flexibility, with the litmus test being ***what results are we achieving?***

It is important that your people understand WHAT you are doing and HOW this will support THEIR success to open the door for continuous improvement through focused actions.

Exercise: Compile a list of ways you support sales success in your business

**Take action
Complete this** 👉

Some ways that you may support sales enablement are below. Feel free to add your own:

- Sales training
- Competitor intelligence
- Events and trade shows
- Onboarding training
- Coaching
- Buyer persona profiles
- Sales collateral and relevant content
- LinkedIn and social media
- Cross sell and upsell generation
- Benchmarks

- CRM
- Pipeline and activity management
- Product and service training
- Website development
- Strategic alliances
- Lead generation
- Sponsorships
- Press releases
- Referral fees
- Channel partners
- Analytics
- Prospecting strategy

- Branding
- General messaging
- KPIs and reporting
- Role play and practice
- Customer service standards
- Case studies
- Infographics and proposal development
- Online reviews
- Customer satisfaction surveys
- Positioning and pricing

- Direct mail/ email marketing

- Tech stack

- Script

- Lead follow-up

"Successful people do what unsuccessful people are not willing to. Don't wish it was easier; wish you were better. Only then does it become easier."

– Jim Rohn

SETTING YOURSELF UP FOR SUCCESS – MINDSET & ATTITUDES

What is it?

Your Sales Playbook should provide clarity around your expectations on not only tasks but also attitudes and behaviours. It is a good idea to define the qualities that you are looking for or perhaps ask the team what they see as positive attributes amongst the people they enjoy working with.

Why does it matter?

Setting your expectations is a way of making the intangible tangible. We can all think of people who display positive qualities – as well as those who clearly don't – but often we don't put it into words. Our beliefs and attitudes will drive our actions that will create our results. Therefore, success begins with how we think and feel.

Having clearly defined expectations provides the foundation for future performance, one-to-ones, recruitment, and employee development conversations.

Exercise: Characteristics of successful sales people

**Take action
Complete this**

Below are some of the characteristics of high performers. You can use these or create your own based on your team's perception of positive attitudes that drive success.

- **Growth Mindset.** Even if you've worked in sales for many years, there is always something to learn and ways to improve. We can all continually grow and develop by staying open to new concepts.

- **Discipline and Prioritising**. Successful salespeople diligently focus on the activities that matter, every day, without excuses. Great habits drive our success, and each step is important. When we commit to following the process, we create success.

- **Motivation**. While we can provide an inspirational work environment, it is up to you to wake up each day and choose to be your best.

- **Customer Focused.** Without our customers, there can be no business. Our job is to understand their needs, pain points, and challenges in order to help them achieve more of what is important to them through our products and services. Put yourself in their shoes, ask yourself what they want most from you, and deliver it.

- **Build Relationships.** People do business with people they know, like, and trust. Take time to build great relationships internally and externally and connect on a deeper level.

- **Take Care of Your Health.** Your physical, mental, and emotional wellbeing is something that only you can manage. We want you to be able to perform at your best, but this begins with self-care and making your wellbeing a personal priority.

- **Resilience.** There will always be ups and downs in your role and in life. Adopting a resilient mindset means adopting a positive attitude and avoiding taking things too personally. Even if you've had a bad day, there is always tomorrow, and you can start again with a fresh attitude.

- **Personal Responsibility and Accountability.** We are always in control of our own words, actions, and results. If you're struggling with something, reach out and ask for help. Own your role and make it happen.

- **Have Fun.** Happy people are more successful because people find them more engaging and want to talk to them.

- **Care For and Respect Others.** At the core of what we do, we are in the people business. Our emotional intelligence and self-awareness around the impact of our interpersonal relationships are key to our success.

- **Optimism and a Positive Mindset.** Optimistic salespeople outperform pessimists by 57%, even when the pessimists have better sales skills. People like dealing with people who see the bright side of life.

"You will get all you want in life if you help enough other people get what they want."

– Zig Ziglar

FOUR LEVELS OF SALESPEOPLE: WHAT DO WE NEED MOST?

What is it?

Depending on the complexity and value of your services, different sales approaches may be required. The base level is transactional and it is a relatively simple process: it should almost happen on its own. More advanced sales processes will require more steps, relationship-building, technical advice, and on the highest level, a strategic partnership.

Every business has an obligation to provide service to their customers by doing what is requested. This is customer service 101; however, simply waiting for customers to ask will not create a successful business. Similarly, being someone's friend doesn't guarantee that they will want to do business together, not to mention that sometimes too much of a personal connection can get in the way.

Yet we should always strive to have a healthy level of personal connection. We need to be good at what we do and be specialists in our field – always ready to help provide this knowledge to our customers. The pinnacle for salespeople is a strategic partner who proactively supports their customers to succeed in achieving their goals and overcome challenges.

Why does it matter?

To create a truly successful sales team, our people need to embrace all four levels of this approach and understand their role at each step.

Strategic partnerships are truly a case of WIN-WIN-WIN and should be the ultimate goal of every salesperson. This means a WIN for the customer, a WIN for the salesperson, and a WIN for the organisation. To be a true strategic partner, we must focus on helping our client to succeed in what is most important to them by identifying opportunities and challenges that we can help them with. It also means that we need to be good at what we do: experts in our field with reliable advice, support, connections, and relationships. Trust is the foundation which is based on a strong personal relationship with a service mindset.

When we help our customers to succeed, we will build a loyal base of Raving Fans who will provide unlimited returns to our business.

STRATEGIC PARTNER
Identifies goals, challenges and opportunities and helps them succeed

TECHNICAL EXPERT
Supports with specialist advice

RELATIONSHIP BUILDER
Builds a personal connection

ORDER TAKER
Does what they are asked to

Order taker	Relationship builder	Technical expert	Strategic partner
• Does what is asked	• Relationships are everything	• Understands the details of what they need	• Proactive partnership
• Waits for instructions	• Strong personal connection	• Provides specialist advice	• Valued input to help them succeed
• If the client wants it, they'll ask	• Will do whatever is needed to help them	• Experienced industry professional	• Creates loyalty through WIN-WIN-WIN outcomes

Exercise: Four Levels of Salespeople

**Take action
Complete this**

- What does it mean to be in each of these categories?

- Why can we not afford to remain order takers?

- Why doesn't being only a Relationship Builder secure new business opportunities?

- Why does being good at what we do technically not guarantee us new opportunities?

- What does a Strategic Partnership look like in our business, and how does this benefit all parties?

"A brand is not a product or a promise or a feeling. It's the sum of all the experiences you have with a company."

– Amir Kassaei

REPRESENTING YOUR ORGANISATIONAL BRAND

What is it?

Every business has a brand which is created consciously and unconsciously. Your brand is your customer's perception of your business through what they see, hear, feel, and think in relation to doing business with you.

Why does it matter?

Each team member is a Brand Ambassador for your business – conveying who you are, what you stand for, and your capability to your clients. Accordingly, you must present an aligned approach to create consistency across the business. The more everyone feels aligned with your shared values, standards, practices, and behaviours, the more congruent and successful team will be.

Some of the key factors that are important in representing your brand are listed below. You may like to add some of your own:

- Use of approved materials
- Style guides and formatting of documents
- Personal presentation
- Customer service focus

- Responsible alcohol consumption, code of conduct

- Interactions with customers and stakeholders

- How we speak about our competitors or other industry representatives

- Punctuality and preparation

"Your personal brand is what people say about you AFTER you've left the room."

– Naomi Oyston

PERSONAL BRAND

What is it?

We are constantly communicating, and most of this is nonverbal. People feel and notice our vibe within the first four seconds of meeting us, long before we hold a conversation.

It is important to be aware of how others may subconsciously perceive our professionalism and how this impacts their likelihood of choosing to do business with us.

Some factors that others notice are:

- Appearance – clothes, grooming, shoes, hair, neatness, jewellery
- Knowledge and capability
- Time management and punctuality
- Reliability
- Approachability
- Trustworthiness
- Eye contact
- Self-interest and motivation

- Communication style – verbal and written
- Preparation and composure
- Energy levels and mood
- Passion for what we do
- Organisation
- Genuine interest in helping others
- Personality and likeability
- Language used
- Optimism or pessimism

Why does it matter?

You never get a second chance to make a good first impression; your sales success depends on the strength of your personal brand. Human beings make emotional decisions subconsciously and very quickly – almost instantly, in fact – and then rationalise these decisions later on a slower, more logical basis. These principles relate to not only sales but customer service, teamwork, and anywhere that we are required to build interpersonal relationships.

Most of our personal brand is created unconsciously and we are not always aware of how we may come across to others, so it is important to shine a light on the things that people may notice about us but not always tell us.

Exercise: Personal brand – What do people notice about us?

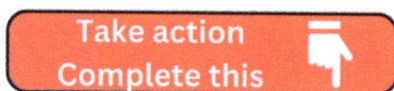

Take action
Complete this

What are the key things we need to be aware of when interacting with team members, customers, or in professional environments? What type of personal brand do we want to intentionally create?

The purpose of an elevator pitch is to describe a situation or solution so compelling that the person you're with wants to hear more even after the elevator ride is over.

– Seth Godin

ELEVATOR PITCH

What is it?

An elevator pitch is a 30-second or less way to introduce yourself when asked, "So what do you do?" A good elevator pitch allows you to share important information quickly. If we think about a ride in an elevator with an important decision-maker who we really want to engage, there is a very short amount of time to share information, capture their attention, get to the point, and create interest for a further discussion or call to action.

In today's world, it's not always about pitching in elevators but more often we may find it helpful to be prepared with our pitch during community events, professional networking opportunities, or even social interactions. Some businesses now call it a BBQ pitch – how would you introduce yourself if you were out at a BBQ, gauging interest in your services from the other guests? First impressions matter and we need a strong introduction that is clear, conversational, and compelling.

Why does it matter?

A powerful elevator pitch will be engaging and pique the listener's curiosity enough for them to ask for more information. A poorly delivered elevator pitch will do the opposite, with most people either being too vague and in general not giving enough OR giving too much information by rambling on about themselves.

We are always interacting with different people, and you never know who might know someone who could be your ideal client.

It pays to be prepared and ready!

Exercise: Create your powerful and engaging elevator pitch

When someone asks "What do you do?", be prepared with a strong response.

A good format for this is:

- You know how to… (describe typical target market and their problem/pain points)

- Well, what we do is… (simple statement about how we help)

- In fact, we've recently helped… (example of a type of client you've helped)

- And what they've found is… (results from working with you)

- Tell me a little more about you… (invitation to learn about each other)

A sample elevator pitch that is aligned with our business is:

Foundations: In summary

1. Your Sales Playbook should begin with building a deep understanding and emotional connection to the WHO, WHY, HOW, WHEN, and WHAT of your organisation. This supports your people to become evangelists who will continue to share your background, vision, purpose, and strengths through their interactions. Your first sale is to your people – from here they can sell you to your customers.

2. To win the marketplace, first you must win the workplace by creating a high-performance sales culture. Culture can be defined as "how we do things around here" and will either be created deliberately by default – you get to choose.

3. You can't manage what you don't measure. Every business needs to define the highest value focus areas to create a Results Dashboard that measures results on a daily, weekly, monthly, quarterly, or annual basis.

4. Success requires a combination of mindset, toolkit and skill set. Your people need to be clear about how to succeed, capable of doing the actions required for success, and confident in their belief systems to take action.

5. There are four levels of salespeople and our goal is to embrace all of these. The base level is the Order Taker where we do what the customer asks. The next is the Relationship Builder where we create a personal connection. We need to have Technical Experts to demonstrate our knowledge and capability in our field. Lastly, to be truly successful in sales, we must become a Strategic Partner where we proactively work together with our clients to achieve their goals, deal with challenges, and maximise opportunities.

6. Your brand is not a product or promise – it's people's perception of the sum of all experiences that they have with you. Brands are built slowly but can be damaged very quickly, so it is important to build awareness and expectations around what is required to represent your brand in a positive light. Just as we have an organisational brand, we also each have a personal brand that will impact the likelihood of others choosing to do business with us – or not.

7. Every person within your business should be ready to share their elevator pitch when they come into contact with potential customers, suppliers, or introducers. This may be in a professional or personal situation as we are always building networks and we never know who knows someone who could use our help. This is a 30-second response when asked "So what do you do?" which should create interest for further discussion.

2:
THE SALES
CYCLE – STRATEGY

"Without strategy, execution is aimless. Without execution, strategy is useless."

– Morris Chang

DEFINING YOUR SALES CYCLE – STRATEGY

What is it?

Your Sales Cycle Strategy is a collection of strategies created to maximise opportunities at each stage of the sales journey.

There are seven distinct steps within a Sales Strategy, and each of these should be defined in more detail throughout your playbook. The goal is to progress your clients throughout the sales cycle until you reach the "pot of gold" by leveraging your satisfied clients (who are now Raving Fans) to create an increasing stream of new business.

Why does it matter?

There are different focuses for each stage of the buying process, and salespeople need to understand what is required at each stage – alongside what not to do.

It should begin with your customer at the centre and focus on what value you provide, how you distinguish yourself from your competitors, and why they should do business with you. This is the foundation of your strategy. Sales is all about delivering value to your customers in a way that meets THEIR needs, not YOURS. As you continue to develop your strategies across all stages, it's important to remain customer-centric to ensure that you are building advocacy throughout.

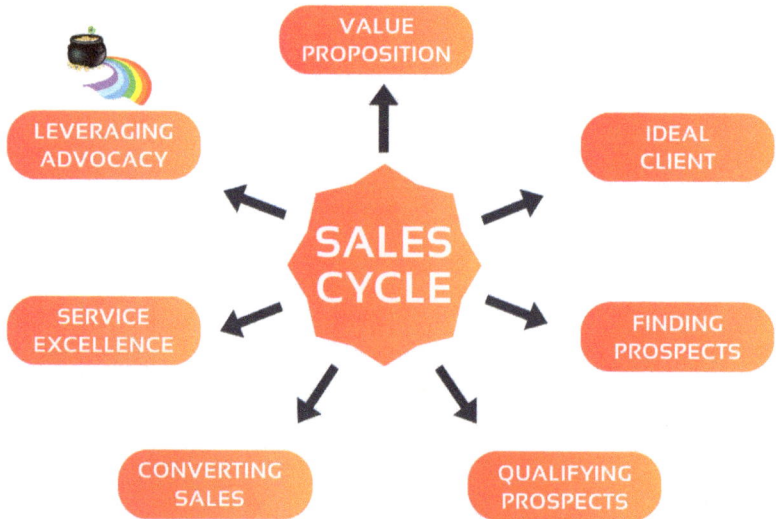

Value Proposition:

- Why should your ideal client choose you?

Ideal Client:

- Who do you most want to do business with?

Finding Prospects:

- Where can we find high value prospects?

Qualifying Prospects:

- How can we discover if this is the right fit?

Converting Sales:

- What may be needed to close?

Service Excellence:

- How can we create Raving Fans?

Leveraging Advocacy:

- How can we generate repeat business and referrals?

In a customer's eyes,
What makes us attractive to buy
from? What problems do we solve?
How do we help with what's
important to them?
How are we different from our
competitors?

VALUE PROPOSITION – WHY US?

What is it?

Your value proposition is the reason that your customers will choose to do business with you – the "What's in it for me?" You should be able to easily articulate the unique benefits and value that you offer, along with how you can solve their problems and avoid pain or increase their opportunities and gain pleasure in a way that differs from your competitors.

Why does it matter?

Your value proposition is one of the most important parts of your sales strategy and must be customer-centred – it is not about what you think but what THEY think that matters. Unless there is a compelling reason to buy and

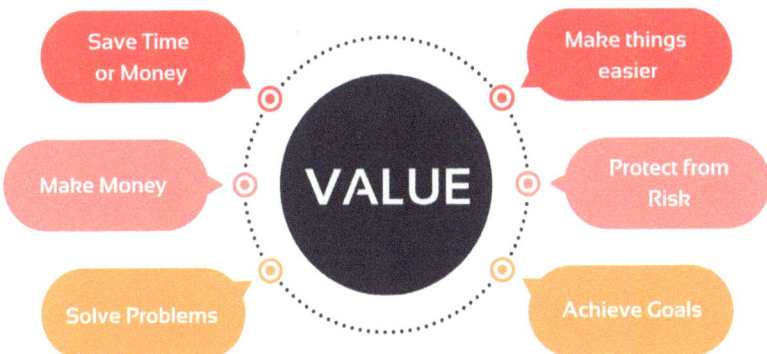

remain with your business beyond price, your customers will never become **Raving Fans**. In the absence of clear value, our customers will be susceptible to offers from competitors or can become simply price-driven by reducing margins and retention. Every salesperson should know how to communicate this in a passionate, customer-focused manner.

Exercise: What Value do we provide for our customers?

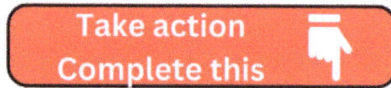

Take action
Complete this

- What are our key products and services?

- What results – tangible and intangible – do our customers get from working with us?

- Who are our major competitors and what is our point of difference?

- What problems do we solve? What is the cost of not having our help and the value of having our help? Where is the pain that we can solve?

- What do our most satisfied clients say about us?

- Why should we be considered a premium provider?

- How would our customers describe us in a referral to another customer?

- Where is our WIN zone?

- What is the value that we bring through industry insights and experience?

Product/ Service	Target market/ Avatar	Problem/ Need	Features, Benefits, and Value

Competitor offerings	Strengths	Weaknesses	How We Win

"Seek first to understand, then be understood."

– Stephen R Covey

IDEAL CLIENT PROFILE

What is it?

Your ideal client profile is a detailed summary of your target customers. This should be based on the type of clients who will achieve maximum value from doing business with you and become Raving Fans. Your ideal client profiles will include attributes such as values, goals, pain points, and purchasing behaviours, which helps you target and discover the right type of prospects.

To do this well, you must dig deeper to learn more about what your ideal customer's real needs are – which may be different from what you think they are – what problems they face; what opportunities may lie ahead if they are successful in their goals; how they feel when dealing with these problems or opportunities; and what they want to achieve most.

Sometimes it is easier to do this with an existing high-value customer in mind: step into their shoes for a moment to consider their perspective and this activity will become simple.

Why does it matter?

Our job is not to sell things to people who don't want or need our products and services but to find the right customers who do truly value what we offer and our relationship with them. Before we can set out to find the right customers, we need to identify who we are looking for and "get inside their head" to understand their position – let's walk a mile in their shoes.

Getting clear about what you're looking for can become much more targeted with your activities and provide a deeper, more meaningful customer experience because your prospects feel like you really understand their world. It helps you to serve your customers better, address their needs and opportunities, while in turn increasing retention and profitability.

Your ideal customer should be:

- High revenue to you, providing high value to them

- In demand of your services; they need you

- Easy to do business with in regards to your core service offerings

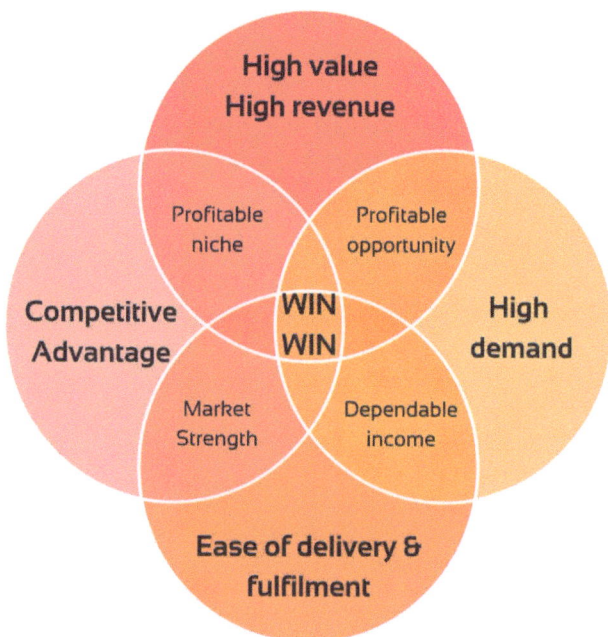

- Able to see you as better than your competitors for their unique needs

Exercise: Ideal Client Profile

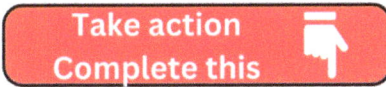

**Take action
Complete this**

- Who do we most want to do business with when considering revenue, industry, headcount, budget, geography, budget, and maturity?

- What are the traits of an ideal client? What are their attitudes, skills, communication, financial capability, technology, location, and buyer persona?

- How do we assess or score the lead to see if they are the right prospect for us?

- What do they really, really want from us? What are their deepest desires?

- What are their pain points or challenges regarding finances, productivity, process, capability, and reputation that we can help with?

- What other key priorities are they dealing with?

- What is their worst-case scenario in dealing with us – their unspoken fear of buying?

- What information do we need to obtain initially to ascertain if there is a good fit?

- Who are the major stakeholders or influencers who will be involved in the decision-making process?

- What other options could they be considering other than ours?

- Why do they need us?

- Where is our WIN- zone when considering high demand, ease of delivery, competitive advantage, and high value and revenue?

"Every person in your business can (and should) prospect for new opportunities as we all have different strengths.
The Hunter, the Farmer, and the Fisherman each bring value through their personal interactions and centres of influence."

– Naomi Oyston

FINDING PROSPECTS

What is it?

Every business needs to have a robust lead generation process to create a pipeline of new sales opportunities. Finding new prospects is a very important piece of the Sales Strategy and will generally require a multi-faceted approach, taking into account:

- Urgency or need to purchase

- Stage in the buying cycle (from building awareness through to ready-to-buy)

- Level of trust in place

- Size of the investment required

- Cost and complexity of lead generation

- Alternatives available to our prospects

Why does it matter?

Sales prospecting helps you to identify potential new customers who have an interest or need aligned with your solutions. Quality prospecting will create viable opportunities, ideally with a short lead time and ease of conversion.

Interestingly, a report from RAIN Group reported that more than 7 out of 10 buyers want to hear from salespeople early in their buying process and 82% of buyers will accept a meeting when the salesperson reaches out first. Yet prospecting is very often one of the key activities that salespeople avoid. Unproductive prospecting, when it's either not targeted or not managed professionally, is a huge time waster and disheartening for all involved. This tends to diminish the desire to do more, perpetuating the beliefs that it is not a high-value use of our time and resources.

Types of Behaviour That Drive Sales Opportunities

THE HUNTER **ACQUISITION**	THE FARMER **RETAIN AND GROW**	THE FISHERMAN **ATTRACT**
• Hunts for new opportunities • Acts independently • Quick to connect and assess fit • Motivated by the win • Competitive and persistent • Moves on when deal is done • Short term focus	• Fosters and nurtures relationships • Team player • Focused on customers needs • Motivated by helping • Collaborative and service oriented • Grows revenue by WIN WIN • Long term focus	• Attracts interest with "bait" • Knows where to fish • Understands prospects needs • Marketing for customer journey • Strategic and informed • Creates strong content and process • Ongoing focus

The truth is that everyone can prospect, but we may go about it in different ways when we feel clear and confident in our approach. Three types of behaviours drive sales opportunities. Great sales teams have a balance of all three and recognise the importance of working together to generate new leads.

The Hunter: Acquisition - Seeks out new opportunities and closes deals

Hunters generally act independently, are motivated by the win and are very competitive. They tend to have a relatively short-term focus and will move on to the next opportunity quickly after they've closed a deal. They feel confident contacting prospects and pitching their services. They love the thrill of the chase and will be persistent in overcoming challenges to win the deal. Hunters enjoy building relationships that could benefit their mutual success.

Traits: Outgoing, innovative, big picture (less attention to detail), risk takers and comfortable with rejection.

The Farmer: Retain and Grow - Nurtures relationships for future opportunities

Farmers are traditionally team players who love to HELP others. They enjoy building relationships and are focused on meeting their customer's needs. Farmers are collaborative, motivated by helping their customers, delivering excellent service and value. They cultivate long-term relationships to retain and grow accounts with a proven track record of reliability. Farmers grow business revenue through WIN-WIN support aligned to the organisational and customer's needs.

Traits: Organised with a good attention to detail, caring, patient, good listeners and dislike feeling "pushy" so prefer to help rather than sell.

The Fisherman: Attracts – Draws interest through marketing and specialist knowledge

Fisherman use a "pull" rather than "push" sales strategy by attracting opportunities to them through using the right bait and knowing where to fish. They understand their prospect's needs and create strategic, high value content to draw the prospect to them throughout the customer journey. They have a deep understanding of marketing and content creation to attract the opportunity, qualify and deliver value along the way.

Traits: Analytical, strategic, innovative, great story tellers and strong communicators to focus on what works.

While the Hunter seeks the thrill of new opportunities, the Farmer tends to the field of existing clients and the Fisherman attracts new prospects to the table.

Exercise: Best Practices That Drive New Business

Within your business, there will be unlimited opportunities to prospect, and as a team you can identify multiple strategies and the highest value focus areas for each role with clear expectations around the quality and quantity of activity required.

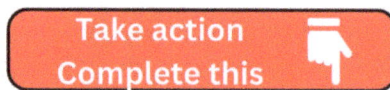

> **Take action**
> **Complete this** 👆

- Cold calling / warm calling with a personal introduction

- Existing clients – repeat business

- Client referrals

- Research intelligence (eg New project announced)

- Marketing and lead generation

- Centres of influence – referral partners and personal connections

- Previous clients

- Trade shows

- LinkedIn connections / advertising / newsletters

- Trigger events or market conditions that signify a potential need

- Networking groups

- Upsell of additional products and services to existing clients

- Influencers – similar circles but different business focus

- WIN-WIN relationships (eg Another supplier providing complementary solutions to you where you can work together to provide a full service)

- Community involvement and sponsorships

- Targeted connections (eg Previously quoted but didn't proceed)

Leveraging LinkedIn

LinkedIn launched in 2003 and has grown to be the largest professional social network globally, with a mission to "Connect the world's professionals to make them more productive and successful." Through LinkedIn, we can network, post content, and connect with prospective clients, advocates, or introducers.

It is a powerful resource and will support our sales activities on many levels, given that:

- Audiences that are exposed to brand messages on LinkedIn are more likely to convert

- 78% of people are using LinkedIn on their phone

- 92% of buyers are interested in engaging with an industry thought leader who shares quality content

- 16% of users are active daily

- Articles (31%), photos (27%), and text posts (25%) are the most popular forms of content shared

- As of June 2023, LinkedIn had more than 930 million members across 200+ countries (13+ million in Australia), adding 60 million new members in the year prior

- Decision-makers use LinkedIn content to vet organisations, with 64% of respondents considering thought leadership to be a reliable way to assess capabilities of a provider

Getting the most out of LinkedIn

- Write your profile with your ideal customer in mind

- Be easy to contact by including your email or website links throughout your profile

- Don't try to sell on LinkedIn; instead, aim to become a trusted advisor and relationship builder

- Send voice messages rather than just written ones – it's a great way to stand out and makes a more personal impact

- Position yourself as an authority in your field

- Share articles and updates that are appropriate to your segment

- Be an advocate for your business by sharing group posts

- Personalise your LinkedIn activity – be human and friendly

- Promote others, show gratitude, find ways to celebrate and recognise success, and share content – givers gain, and people love helping those who help them

- Engage in your network – like or comment on people's posts; recognise occasions (birthdays, work anniversaries, new roles, awards); people pay attention to people who pay attention to them

- When inviting someone to connect with you, make it personal by including a short note

- Ask for recommendations and endorsements

- Have at least 50 connections (it makes you more desirable to connect with if you're active)

- Actively grow your network

- Ask every new person you meet to connect

- Join groups that are appropriate for your industry and actively contribute OR create your own group and invite others to join

- Include a link to your LinkedIn profile in your email, inviting others to connect

- Set a time in your calendar to engage in LinkedIn a minimum of twice per week

- Aim to give value through your content and messages

- Show your personality – balance personal and professional appropriately

- Identify key targets and connect with them

- Consider paid options on LinkedIn – advertising, premium, sales navigator, or recruiter

Exercise: How can we utilise LinkedIn to build relationships and drive sales success through new opportunities?

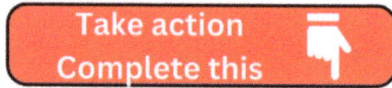

Take action
Complete this

Ways that we can better leverage LinkedIn as a team are:

67% of lost sales are due to ineffective qualifying in the initial needs analysis conversation.

82% of B2B decision-makers think sales reps are unprepared.

(Source: SPOTIO Sales Software)

QUALIFYING PROSPECTS

What is it?

When we have uncovered a potential prospect, we must have a process to understand if they are a good fit – or not. We are not doing anyone favours by trying to fit a square peg in a round hole; we must first have a quality conversation to identify our prospect's actual needs and if our solution is appropriate for what they want and need.

A quality needs-based conversation is not about "selling" but instead "understanding". It allows us to uncover potential solutions or challenges to enable us to do business. People are most likely to be open to influence if they feel heard and understood.

A good approach for lead qualification is "scoring" based on the attributes of your ideal client. This can guide your

NEEDS BASED CONVERSATION

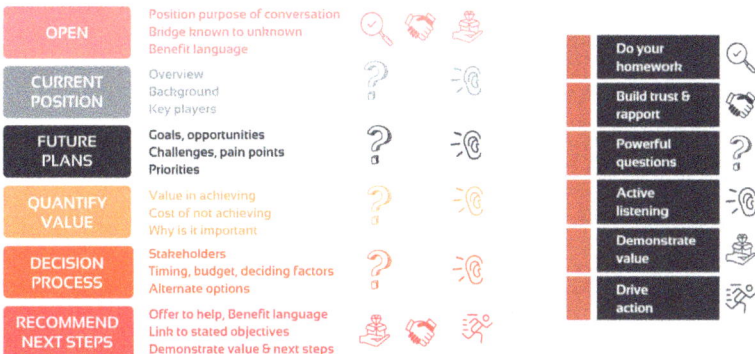

OPEN	Position purpose of conversation Bridge known to unknown Benefit language	
CURRENT POSITION	Overview Background Key players	
FUTURE PLANS	Goals, opportunities Challenges, pain points Priorities	
QUANTIFY VALUE	Value in achieving Cost of not achieving Why is it important	
DECISION PROCESS	Stakeholders Timing, budget, deciding factors Alternate options	
RECOMMEND NEXT STEPS	Offer to help, Benefit language Link to stated objectives Demonstrate value & next steps	

Do your homework	
Build trust & rapport	
Powerful questions	
Active listening	
Demonstrate value	
Drive action	

needs-based conversations to understand their position at the forefront.

Why does it matter?

A good no is a quick no! Every opportunity that we work on should be qualified as quickly as possible with an aim to move to the next step in the sales process. Otherwise, we can end up inflating our pipeline with deals that are never going anywhere, wasting time for both ourselves and our prospects. Worse still, this also potentially causes brand reputational damage from being a company who has messed around a prospect and not been able to deliver a satisfactory solution. Just as we want to make sure that we do everything we can to win the right deals, we should also eliminate the wrong deals as quickly as possible to enable us to focus on other opportunities.

When we ask well-prepared quality questions, our prospects will feel understood and that we are professionals in our approach.

A quality needs-based conversation contains a clear structure, powerful questions, value propositions, and action steps. Prospects do not care about your product or service; they care most about resolving their pain or realising their rewards, so they should do 80% of the talking throughout the process. When we get this conversation right, our prospects feel heard, understood, and respected. We also get a clear picture of the likelihood of this opportunity proceeding – so we can spend more time on deals we can win.

Our success in converting opportunities is amplified when we have a solid needs-based conversation.

Understand the past ⬅	*Drive actions* now ⬇	*Sell* the future ➡

Exercise: Preparing for a Needs-Based Sales Conversation

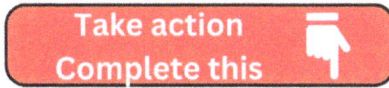

**Take action
Complete this** 👆

Create a best practice question guide for each of the above areas based on buyer persona, pain points, needs, and opportunities.

Pre-meeting planning – do some homework

- Website review – what's important on their website?
- What do we know? What do we need to know?
- What do we need to get them talking about?
- What is the purpose of our meeting?
- Why may our prospect not want to buy from us, and how can we prepare for this?

Open

- Build trust and rapport with a personal connection
- Share your elevator pitch if appropriate
- Have a clear purpose for the conversation (not to "have a chat" and "see where it goes")

- Use benefit language to introduce the conversation (I understand you've got some impressive opportunities coming up and want to see if we can streamline the process to be more profitable for you.)

Current position

- Background of the client
- Stakeholders or key players
- Size of business
- Service offerings
- Ideal clients and projects
- Strengths of the business

Future plans

- Goals for the future – long- and short-term
- Opportunities identified
- What's most important?
- What does success look like?
- Potential challenges or pain points

Quantify value

- What is the value of achieving these goals?
- What is the cost of not achieving these goals?
- Why does this matter?
- What else does this allow you to do?

Decision process

- Is there a budget in place?
- Who are the key decision-makers?

- What do they need to know? What could their concerns be?

- Are there any other options you're considering?

- For this to work, what would you need to see?

- What is your decision process and timing?

- Is there a procurement process?

Recommendation and next steps

- Thank them for any information shared

- Ask if there's anything important that you haven't already talked about

- Confirm that you have a good understanding of where they're at and where they want to be

- Tell them you'd like to help with a benefit statement (I've got some great ideas about how I might make this whole process more efficient for you, and I'd love to help you achieve your goals.)

- Introduce recommendations with links to goals

- Check for engagement, any questions, confirm interest

- Clear next steps and actions required

"The short course in selling: Ask questions and listen. Stop showing up and throwing up. Help them with what is important to THEM! Success is in the palm of your hand, reach for it!"

– Jack Daly

CONVERTING PROSPECTS

What is it?

After we've created a pipeline of qualified prospects through our needs-based conversations, we must have strategies in place to nurture and convert into closed business wherever possible.

Closing a deal is not about aggressive sales tricks but rather supporting the right type of prospects through the buying process. Winning the business is a reward for understanding your clients and confidently demonstrating the value you bring to them.

Closing should be a natural progression if you are gaining agreement at each stage throughout the process as you move them to the next stage. This means you may not close a deal in the first contact, and there could be several steps as they progress through the pipeline.

At each stage, it is an opportunity for us to reinforce how our solution creates value for them.

Why does it matter?

This is one of the most important parts of the sales process. It's essential that we can anticipate and prepare for any potential resistance or delays that may come up. This may take the form of objections, misunderstandings, comparisons to other providers, existing supplier relationships, pricing disagreements, or stakeholder misalignment.

Objection Management

While it might seem like there is no end to possible blocks to closing, there are only really five objections that a prospect may have in doing business with us:

- Money (too expensive; can't afford it)

- Need or Desire (nice to have but don't need or want it)

- Trust (can you be relied upon to do what you say you will?)

- Time or Urgency (too busy; not a priority right now)

- Experience with your Business (previously been let down – what's different now?)

The above objections are universal across multiple businesses and industries and can generate a fear of making the wrong decision for our buyer, which results in inertia or not moving forward. Often these objections are

Features tell, Benefits sell,
Value will compel

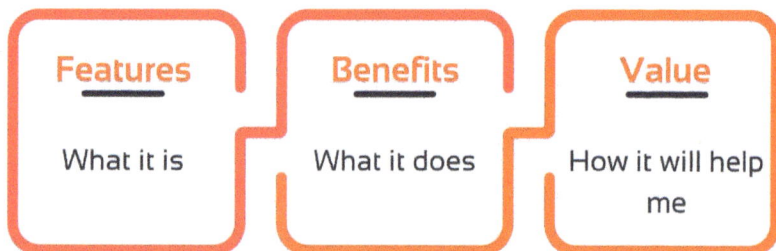

Features	Benefits	Value
What it is	What it does	How it will help me

an opportunity for us to understand a little more about what's really behind the response, so a good response is, "Tell me more about that. Can you help me to understand what pricing you were expecting or would work for you?"

If we have had a quality needs-based conversation, can demonstrate true value in our solutions, and understand their decision criteria, closing will become the next natural step.

Closing Techniques

People don't want to be sold to, but they do love being helped to buy a valued solution. The days of using the hard closing techniques are long gone – these days prospects can smell it a mile away. Instead, we need to focus on using soft closing techniques where the buyer feels empowered of their own free will to move forward.

Some examples of soft closing techniques are:

- DIRECT: Are you happy with everything? Shall we go ahead? Are you ready to get moving now?

- ASSUMPTIVE: When would you expect to have the signed agreement back to me?

- RECIPROCITY: Would you be ready to move ahead if I can get you XYZ (insert what they want)?

- REVERSE: So we've talked about lots of ways that we can help you, and you can see the process ahead. What do we need to do to make this happen now? Is there anything else we need to discuss before we put this into place for you?

- OPINION: I understand that you'll need to talk this through with some other people involved in your decision. Do you think they'll be happy to proceed based on what we've discussed? Is there anything we need to discuss further to ensure they're comfortable?

- HYPOTHETICAL: If you were to proceed, when would you be ready to start this?

- URGENCY: We discussed that your XYZ needs to be in place by XYZ date. If we make that happen, I'll need your decision by the end of the week – are you OK with that? I'm keen to get this started as soon as possible. The longer you leave it, the longer it will take. If you can commit to this by XYZ date, I can get it ready to get started by XYZ date.

- COMMITMENT: When we spoke, you mentioned that this is a key priority and something you're currently focusing on. Can we get this into place and make life a little easier for you to move on to the other areas you also need to manage?

- COMPARATIVE: I think that covers my recommendations. How does that compare with any other options you've looked at? What/where/who else would you be comparing our services to?

- HOW FAR APART? OK – that surprises me because I'm constantly being told that we're really competitive with our pricing in the market that we play in. How far apart are we? What are the differences in what you're comparing us to?

- SIMPLICITY: I want to make this as easy as possible for you to go ahead with. What do you need from me to make it simple for you to get this happening?

- HOW SERIOUS: On a scale of 1 to 10, how serious are you about taking action? If less than an 8, what is holding you back from deciding and stepping forward? If it's a 9 or 10, it sounds like it's time to get this in place. Let's do XYZ to get started.

- IF NOT NOW, THEN WHEN? So when would be a good time to decide? What is it that you're waiting for? How much longer are you prepared to wait?

- ELIMINATE MONEY CONCERN: Would you be ready to get started if this was free? If this is purely a financial concern, let's talk about options.

- FEEL, FELT, FOUND: I understand how you feel. Some of our other clients have felt like that as well; however, they've found that once they've made the decision and things are moving, they felt a huge sense of relief, and things became easy for them.

Exercise: Create best practice responses for common objections

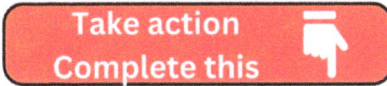

> Take action
> Complete this

Best practice responses for the below:

What they say	What else could this mean?	Best practice response
	MONEY	
	NEED OR DESIRE	
	TRUST	
	TIME OR URGENCY	
	PREVIOUS BAD EXPERIENCE	

The top 10 most common objections that we may encounter along with best practice responses are:

What they say	Best practice responses

"Your objective is to continue to build trust, add value, and move the prospect to the next step..."

– Naomi Oyston

PIPELINE MANAGEMENT

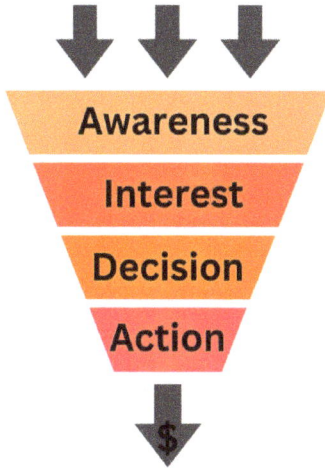

What is it?

Understanding and managing our sales pipeline of opportunities is essential to our success. We must have a clear picture of what prospects we are working on, which stage of the sales process they are at, and how we can move them to the next step within the sales process.

Effective CRM usage can boost sales and productivity by up to 30%, so quality in = quality out.

Why does it matter?

To understand the real value of a sales pipeline, we need to consider how likely each opportunity is to progress to a sale. In simple terms, an enquiry is worth a lot less than a contract issued. Our goal throughout the pipeline process is to help the prospect move to the next step, increasing their value or likelihood of closing.

The most effective way to forecast sales figures is to use a "weighted" pipeline management process where the percentage of the total opportunity increases as it gets closer to fulfilment.

Example: There is a new opportunity for a $100,000 deal. The value of the opportunity increases as we progress it to the next level.

Stage	Weighting	Value
1. Prospect identified	0%	$ 0
2. Contact made to discuss potential	5%	$ 5,000
3. Need identified	10%	$ 10,000
4. Demonstration / pitch presented	20%	$ 20,000
5. Proposal issued	30%	$ 30,000
6. Proposal accepted	65%	$ 65,000
7. Contracts issued	85%	$ 85,000
8. Contracts returned and correct	95%	$ 95,000
9. Settled	100%	$100,000

The best-practice sales strategy is to have a total weighted value of around 12 weeks of sales target in the pipeline at any point in time.

Using a weighted pipeline assists with the following:

- Visibility into the progress of opportunities and the likehood of closing

- Taking the most appropriate actions to move them to the next step

- Understanding where prospects are stalling or dropping off

- Creating accurate forecasting of future results

- Improving efficiency and effectiveness in the most important areas

- Greater focus on high-value opportunities

- Higher close rates

- Benchmarking performance and activity levels

At each touchpoint, we should aim to keep the lead warm and add value wherever possible.

Sales Statistics

48% *of salespeople never follow up with a prospect*
25% *make a second contact and stop*
17% *stop after the third contact*
10% *of salespeople make more than three contacts*

2% *of sales are made on the first contact*
3% *are made on the second contact*
5% *are made on the third*
10% *are made on the fourth*
80% *are made on the fifth to twelfth contact*

Source: National Sales Executive Association

Exercise: Pipeline management techniques

**Take action
Complete this**

- What are the various stages of our prospect's buying journey?

- What might their considerations, concerns, or needs be at each stage?

- How can we continue to build trust and deliver value throughout?

- How will we create momentum in our pipeline to avoid stalled opportunities?

- Where are the blockages in our sales pipeline now and how can we improve this?

- How frequently should we be making contact at each stage of the pipeline?

"*Let us never negotiate out of fear,*
but let us never fear to negotiate."

– John F Kennedy

NEGOTIATION

What is it?

Negotiation is a process where two or more parties arrive at an outcome through compromising to reach an agreement that is acceptable and beneficial for all. The process begins with each party sharing their needs and wants to build a baseline understanding of each other's position. There should also be a clear intention that you want to reach a place where both parties feel happy and ready to proceed through a WIN-WIN approach. Before going into a serious negotiation, we should be aware of our best alternatives if we are not able to reach an agreement.

Negotiation is very common in sales, and it is a skill that should be embraced rather than avoided.

Why does it matter?

In sales, there will often be a gap between what the seller and the customers want. This may be pricing but it could also be terms and conditions, risks, quality, or support levels. Our goal is to reach terms and conditions that both your business and your customer will accept.

Depending on the complexity of your services, there could be many different scenarios.

A simple framework for the stages of negotiation is:

1. **Preparation** – Researching the issues, interests, needs, and positions of the other party

2. **Open discussion** – Sharing information about what's important to them and making an initial case for their side

3. **Clarification of goals** – Identifying highest priorities and common interests

4. **Negotiation** – Each making concessions to foster good faith and commitment to WIN-WIN

5. **Agreement** – Each party takes responsibility for implementing their part of the agreement in order to move forward

Exercise: Negotiation opportunities

**Take action
Complete this**

- What are the most common aspects that we need to negotiate on to close a sale?

- Apart from price, what do our customers want from us?

- Where is the distance between "Aspirational" and "Acceptance" for both parties?

- What would our best alternative offers look like?

- How can we increase the value without decreasing the price?

- What levers do both parties have?

- If we accept less than the original request, what value can we ask for in return?

"Service excellence is the most effective marketing tool you will ever have – through this we produce Raving Fans who will do the selling for us and help us to grow our business faster than we ever could alone."

– Naomi Oyston

SERVICE EXCELLENCE: CREATING RAVING FANS

What is it?

The purpose of an organisation is to create highly satisfied customers. Our ability to create and deliver a high-quality experience is the core of the business – without customers, we have no business.

Customer satisfaction is a leading indicator of how likely they are to purchase from us again or refer others to us.

Drivers of Customer Satisfaction

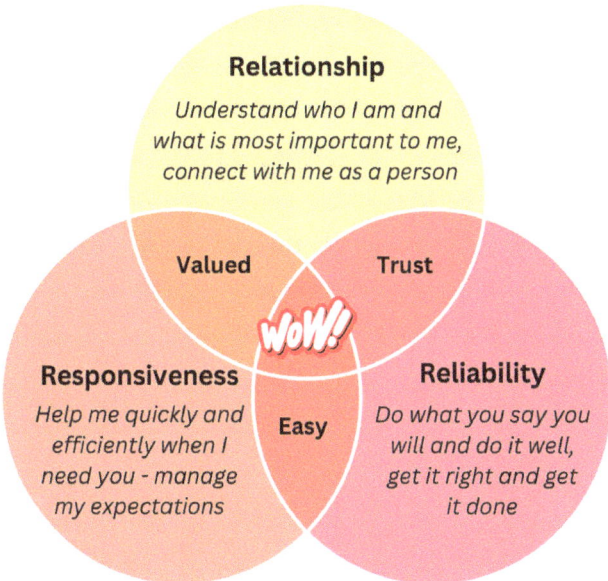

Relationship

Understand who I am and what is most important to me, connect with me as a person

Valued

Trust

WoW!

Responsiveness

Help me quickly and efficiently when I need you - manage my expectations

Easy

Reliability

Do what you say you will and do it well, get it right and get it done

- Speed of service

- Knowledgeable help

- Convenience and ease of doing business

- Reliability

- Providing valued solutions

- Personal connection and friendly service

- Willingness to help

Why does it matter?

It makes good business sense to master this process as it will:

- Increase the lifetime value of the customer

- Provide a true differentiator from competitors

- Increase the number of qualified referrals

- Reduce the acquisition costs of new customers

- Reduce churn and customer runoff, thereby increasing retention

- Protect our reputation and reduce negative word-of-mouth

- Reduce the price sensitivity on future business

- Increase the ease of doing business

- Reduce costs of doing business and increase profitability

- Create **Raving Fans** who promote our business for us

Referrals from Raving Fans...

16%
higher
lifetime
value

30%
higher
conversion
rate

37%
higher
retention
rate

4
times more
likely to
refer others

Exercise: How can we create Raving Fans?

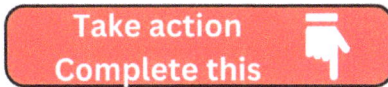

**Take action
Complete this**

- What is a Raving Fan in our business, and how can they help us?

- What would create a 10/10 WOW experience above base expectations?

- How do we measure customer experience and ensure they are satisfied throughout their journey?

- What do our most satisfied customers like best about dealing with us?

- What are the issues that arise that can create dissatisfaction? How can we anticipate or prepare for this?

- What are the key things we need to get right every time?

- What is our complaint management process? Where do we drop the ball?

- How can we better anticipate and prepare for our customers' needs?

- How can our reputation suffer if we get this wrong? What is the impact?

- How do we retain, grow, and develop existing customers?

- What additional service could we provide for our top-tier customers?

"91% of customers say they'd give referrals, only 11% ask."

(Source: Dale Carnegie Study)

LEVERAGING ADVOCACY

What is it?

When effectively leveraged, a satisfied customer is one of the most powerful ways of driving future business. These clients represent the "pot of gold" at the end of the rainbow. We have done the hard work to secure the business and we have fulfilled our customer's needs – so the next logical step in the sales process is to leverage the power of our relationships to generate new business opportunities.

Like attracts like: if the client we are dealing with is the right fit for our business, it is very likely that they will also know other people who could be the right fit for us too. Personal referrals have the highest conversion rates, retention, and profitability, since there is an existing level of trust and connection through the mutual party relationship.

Our highly satisfied client may also have additional needs that are being fulfilled by other providers. This is our chance to ask for a greater share of the wallet – or better yet – to look after ALL of their business.

One of the most valuable ways our satisfied customers can help us is offering feedback around what we are doing well, what we could do better, and how we compare to our competitors and industry insights. This information helps us to continually improve and fine-tune our offerings to the market.

Why does it matter?

When we've followed all the steps in the Sales Cycle Strategy, we have done the work required to create a highly satisfied customer and have earned the right to ask for referrals or more business.

While most people recognise that the most cost-effective way to grow a business is through referrals, the reality is that it just doesn't always happen.

This can be for a variety of reasons, including:

- Waiting too long to ask for a referral (beyond the pivotal moments or points of delight)
- Asking for referrals at the wrong time or before delivering a valuable outcome
- Not earning the right to ask
- Asking in an indirect or unconfident manner
- Only asking once and then assuming they don't know anyone
- Not making it easy to be referred to
- Having an ad hoc approach when asking for referrals
- Not providing a benefit or reason for people to refer

Exercise: Generating additional business from customer advocacy

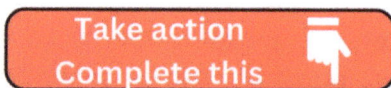

**Take action
Complete this** 👆

- What must we do first to earn the right to ask for more?

- When is the best time to check in for satisfaction (point of power)?

- How can we increase the depth of our relationship through additional products or services (cross sell and upsell)?

- How do we ask for a testimonial or review?

- How do we ask for a referral?

- Would our customers be willing to act as a referee for other prospects?

- How do we connect with their centres of influence or network?

- What other industry insights or advice might our client be able to provide for us?

- How can we use our customer's feedback and insights to improve our sales or marketing process?

"Storytelling is the most powerful way to put ideas into the world today."

– Robert McKee

CASE STUDIES AND SUCCESS STORIES

What is it?

Case studies and success stories should be shared with our prospects to build trust and demonstrate value. Ideally, our prospects should be able to see themselves in the stories we share and feel confident that they can achieve similar outcomes through working with us.

There are two different formats for these: case studies appeal to the left brain or logic and are typically documented; in contrast, success stories are usually spoken and appeal to the right brain or emotion. When

Left Brain

Logic
Analysis
Organisation
Details
Systems
Facts
Risk

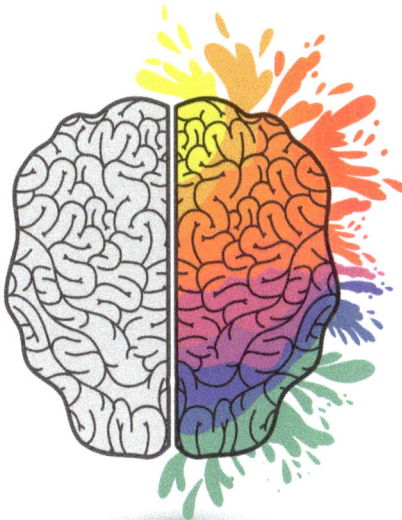

Right Brain

Emotion
Intuition
Big picture
Possibilities
Interpersonal
Flow
Creativity

we combine both sides, we substantially improve the likelihood of compliance because people can understand and feel the impact of working with us.

The format for a case study or success story should be as follows, remembering SPARE:

S = Situation before dealing with us

P = Problem or pain points – what was the cost of this?

A = Action taken to support this

R = Result achieved – what was the benefit of this?

E = Emotion – how did this feel throughout the process?

Why does it matter?

Our goal throughout the sales process is to build trust and demonstrate value. Whilst there are many things that we can say about how capable we are, our prospects are more likely to feel confident in the process if they know others have had a good experience in dealing with us.

One of the principles of influence in sales is social proof. Essentially, this means that if other people who, like me, have had a good experience, then I will feel more confident to make a decision to proceed. This is one of the reasons why online reviews are so important as 77% of people regularly read online reviews before making a decision on a business.

Every business should have a series of case studies and success stories to demonstrate different aspects of their service offerings and use them as appropriate to build trust and show the value that others have experienced through dealing with us.

Exercise: Creating case studies and success stories

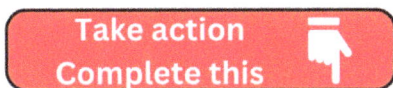

**Take action
Complete this**

The case studies and success stories that can support our business include:

Target customer/ avatar	Pain point/ opportunity	Our services	Result achieved

Which situations should be documented in a case study and which should be used as success stories to share with our prospects?

The Sales Cycle: In summary

Your Sales Strategy is created through seven distinct stages of the sales cycle, and each has its own strategy.

Stage 1 is Value Proposition:

- What is it that you bring to the market?

- Why should your customers choose you?

- How are you different from your competitors?

- What value do you provide?

Stage 2 is Ideal Client Profile:

- Who do you most want to do business with?

- What are the traits of your ideal client?

- What are their pain points or challenges that you can help them with?

- What do they most want or need from you?

Stage 3 is Finding Prospects:

- How do we build a quality pipeline of opportunities?

- Who else deals with our prospects?

- How can we combine the strategies of Hunting (acquisition), Farming (growth through relationship management), and Fishing (attracting leads)?

- Where is there the greatest urgency, level of trust, and readiness to buy?

Stage 4 is Qualifying Prospects:

- Is this prospect the right fit for our business – or not?

- What is it that we need to understand about them?

- How can we structure a needs-based conversation?

- What research or preparation should we be doing prior to meeting with them?

Stage 5 is Converting Prospects:

- We need to actively create a pipeline of opportunities and progress them to the next step.

- What are the potential blockers to closing and how can we prepare for these?

- What influencing or persuasion techniques would support us?

- How can we close the business more efficiently?

Stage 6 is Service Excellence:

- We are not closing business but opening a relationship.

- Reliability, relationships, and responsiveness are the key drivers in customer satisfaction.

- Our goal is to create Raving Fans.

- Customer service is not a department – but it is everybody's job. If you're not serving a customer, you're serving someone who is a customer.

Stage 7 is Leveraging Advocacy:

- Raving Fans are the "pot of gold" at the end of the sales cycle.

- Satisfied customers are happy to give referrals, testimonials, introductions, insights, and feedback.

- We've earned the right to ask for more.

- How can we cross sell, upsell, or gain a greater share of wallet?

3:
PUTTING IT INTO ACTION

"We are what we repeatedly do.
Excellence therefore is not an act,
but a habit."

– Aristotle

HIGH PAYOFF ACTIVITY HABITS

RESULTS =

$$\frac{\text{Quantity x Quality x Consistency}}{\text{Activity}}$$

What is it?

Great salespeople don't just "wing it" when it comes to creating results that matter. They are prepared; they have a plan; they have practised and prioritised their high-value activities. The most effective salespeople are not necessarily the ones who work the hardest but those who know what works and do it consistently.

Sales results are a direct correlation of:

- How much activity we do
- How well we do the activity
- How consistently we do the activity

High payoff activities will generally relate to the seven key areas of selling:

1. Prospecting
2. Relationship building and connection
3. Identifying needs

4. Presenting solutions and asking for the business

5. Dealing with objections or concerns

6. Closing the sale

7. Leveraging advocacy: repeat business and referrals

Why does it matter?

Smart salespeople know where to focus their efforts and where NOT to. We can be more successful with less effort in our busy days by prioritising the 20% of highest value activities and doing these consistently well as non-negotiables.

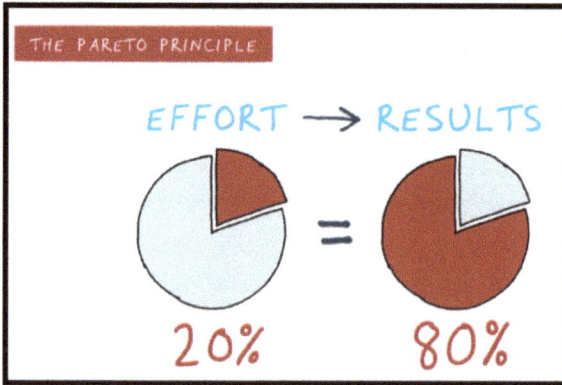

To concentrate on high-value activities, we need to take control of our time in the first instance with excellent calendar management. However, time management alone is not enough to succeed. Avoid feeling rushed, distracted, or unprepared for your day. We must ensure that we are focused and present so that we maintain our energy levels to undertake high-value activities in our peak energy times.

If you don't control your day, your day will control you, and there will always be more to do than hours available. High payoff habits begin with prioritising and are embedded with structure and discipline.

Exercise: Excelling in high payoff activities

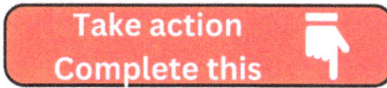

**Take action
Complete this**

- What are the highest value sales activities for each of our roles?

- How can we continually improve the quality, quantity, and consistency of these?

- What are the indicators that we need to improve?

- What would it take for this to be "Business as Usual"?

- How can we maximise our time, focus, and energy habits?

"Psychology is probably the most important factor in the market – and one that is least understood."

– David Dreman

SALES PSYCHOLOGY

What is it?

Sales psychology is a soft skill that is incredibly powerful when mastered. Essentially, it is the study of human behaviour and decision-making processes to define what makes people choose to buy – or not. By understanding the inherent tendencies in human thinking that influence our customer's purchasing decisions, we can enhance our strategies to become more effective in our approach.

Emotions play a significant role in decision-making with most of our reactions being automatic, intuitive, and fast. We then move into logical thinking which is slower, more deliberate, and rational.

"8% of buying decisions are based on logic, while 92% are based on emotions and unconscious bias."

Martin Lindstrom.

Why does it matter?

Understanding sales psychology is not about using sleazy tricks to get people to do what they don't want to, but instead it is about working with both emotion and logic to support the right customers to take action.

Sales psychology helps businesses to:

- Create persuasive marketing messages

- Build rapport and connection

- Tap into emotions and motivations

- Influence decision-making

- Overcome objections and address concerns

- Build confidence in the buying decision

- Develop more meaningful and profitable relationships

Principles of Influence

Following are some principles of influence which, when understood and deliberately applied, have been proven to increase the likelihood of compliance (YES) and reduce resistance (NO).

RECIPROCITY – When I approach every interaction intending to give something of value, I can ethically leverage that feeling into an "obligation" to give me value in return. Givers gain, so I get to earn the right to ask for more.

SOCIAL PROOF – The more I can show you that others, just like you, are taking action that is creating positive outcomes for them, the more likely you will feel inclined also to take aligned action to avoid "missing out" on what others are enjoying.

AUTHORITY – My clients do not want or need to be the expert in every area of their business. They will happily abdicate to my advice or solutions if they feel it removes the complexity from decision-making, AND they see me as the expert in my customers' needs. First, I need to establish that I am the expert.

PROVIDING CHOICE – When we feel like we are making a choice, we feel more empowered rather than being "sold" to. My role is to provide choices aligned with our product or service solution rather than the choice to buy or not to buy through offering "this or that" rather than "yes or no".

PAIN, PLEASURE, and INERTIA – If I can show you that you'll avoid considerable pain or increase pleasure from my solution, you are likely to take action, otherwise your default state will be inertia or not taking action. Moving towards pleasure or away from pain takes more energy than remaining in our comfort zone.

HELP – One of our deepest desires in our interactions is to feel that others are helping us to become more and achieve what is most important to us. If we can show our customers how our solution HELPS them, they are more likely to buy. If our solution doesn't HELP them somehow, it is unlikely to add value.

CONTRAST / COMPARISON – Things make more sense when we compare them, and we are constantly looking for things to compare or contrast to when we make decisions. If I compare my solution to something you understand, you will likely agree it's the best way to go.

COMMITMENT / CONSISTENCY – The more I align my solutions to your objectives or opinions you've stated, the harder it is for you to say no. But first, I must understand your objectives or opinions, then link my solutions to what you've already stated is important.

LIKE, KNOW, and TRUST – The more I connect, the more I find to like about them and the more I show that I genuinely care about them as people rather than sales opportunities. When I build trust through doing what I say I will do, the more they will want to do business with me.

ISSUE PROVOCATION – My product or service is not a solution unless they acknowledge they have a problem and a need, so I need to use great questioning skills to uncover potential issues for the future and agitate the inertia status.

VALUE – People buy because they feel that they will receive more through the exchange of resources. This means if I am paying $100 for something, I need to get more than $100 in value in return to have a return on my investment. The key is that value looks different for different people, so we must first understand what is most important for them.

Exercise: How can we use Sales Psychology to be more successful?

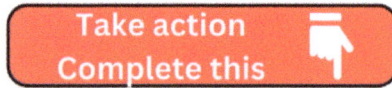

Take action
Complete this

- What techniques make good sense for us to use?

- How can we implement these principles into our customer conversations?

"The ability to understand people is one of the greatest assets anyone can ever have."

– John C Maxwell

ADAPTING TO DIFFERENT PERSONALITY TYPES

What is it?

Regardless of what business you're in, we are all in the people business. One of the core foundations of sales effectiveness is relationship building and to do this well, we need to be able to relate to different types of people who are often within the same room at the same time. Experience has shown that the simplest and most powerful system for understanding people in business is DISC personality assessments. The DISC assessment tool is used by 70% of Fortune 500 companies and thousands of small to medium businesses globally, producing more than 44 million profiles since 1970.

DISC stands for Dominance, Influence, Steadiness, and Compliance which are the four primary ways that people behave. It categorises people into different styles based on their tendencies, preferences, communication styles, motivators, stressors, strengths, and interpersonal dynamics.

Why is it important?

The challenge for salespeople staying in our preferred style is that we will only truly connect with 25% of the population who are also like ourselves. Given that people do business with people they know, like, and trust, it is important that we learn how to relate to others who are not like ourselves to increase our level of influence and drive results. Almost everyone is different, and no style is better than any other. To sell effectively, we need to build rapport and adjust our sales approach to connect with all personality types.

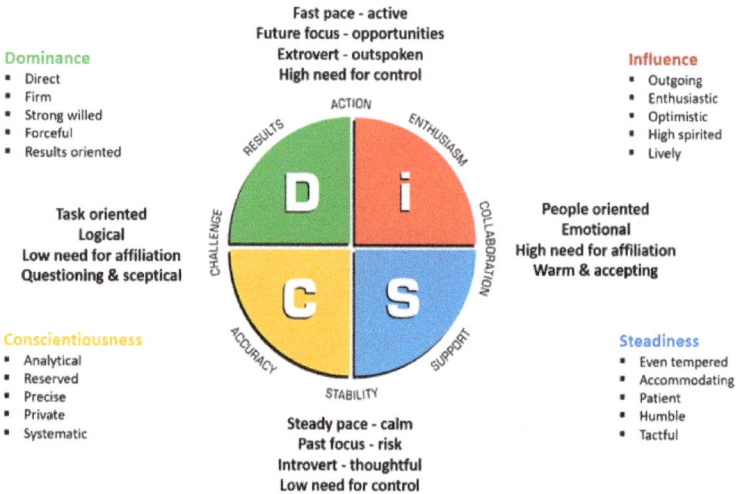

Recognising a D style

Recognising a D style:	
	• Assertive, results-focused, driven
	• Strong-willed
	• No-nonsense attitude
	• Fast-paced, action-oriented
	• Straightforward or blunt way of speaking
	• Willingness to take risks
	• Impatient with small talk

	• Eager to control conversations
	• Quick, decisive
	• Quick to voice opinions
	• Impatient
	• Comfortable with confrontation
	• May overpower or pressure others to get what they need
	• Tends to take charge
What D styles want in a buying experience	• Bottom line results
	• How your solution will help them to be more successful
	• Cut the fluff – don't schmooze
	• Competence, confidence, and can-do attitude
	• Do your homework, and don't expect hand-holding
	• Quick action and forward motion
	• Key points, benefits, and big picture approach – don't get bogged down in detail or analysis
	• Get it right the first time
Pitching to a D	• Provide them with options and empower them to choose
	• Show a desire to help them get immediate results
	• Demonstrate how your offer can improve their bottom line – what's in it for them?

	• Get to the point
	• Create urgency and a rapid pace
	• Be as concise as possible
	• Gain respect by appearing confident and being good at what you do
	• Show respect for their authority
	• Use logic; don't be too emotional
	• Set them up to win
	• Ask what they think
	• Let them see it makes sense to buy
	• FOCUS ON RESULTS

Exercise: How can we adapt our sales process to be more effective with D styles?

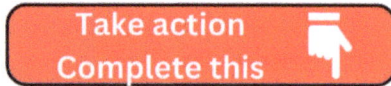

Take action
Complete this

Ways that we can improve our sales process to D styles are:

Recognising an I style

Recognising an I style:	• Fast-paced, outspoken • Accepting, warm; emotional rather than logical • Upbeat and enthusiastic approach • Positive and optimistic outlook • Will share feelings openly • Reliance on intuition, hunches, or gut instinct • Wants to connect and build personal relationships • Considerate of the feelings of others • Eager to meet new people • Tendency to engage in small talk • Willingness to try innovative or creative ideas • Easily distracted when bored • Spontaneous, flexible, excitable • Wants to be liked
What I styles want in a buying experience	• *Enthusiasm, excitement* • *Inspiration to buy* • *Passion, fun* • *Quick action and immediate impact* • *Feelings of motivation and enthusiasm*

	• *Personal relationship – small talk, get to know me, build trust*
	• *Discuss feelings, opinions, and ideas*
	• *Allow the conversation to go where it goes*
	• *Interest in future goals and understanding of what's important*
Pitching to an I	• Highlight the potential and possibilities
	• Be optimistic, upbeat, enthusiastic
	• Get them excited
	• Win them over with compliments
	• Avoid becoming negative, risk-focused, or dampening their enthusiasm
	• Talk about the big picture, dreams, purpose, vision
	• Invite them to talk and share their opinions and feelings
	• Don't give too much detail or analyses
	• Inspire them to buy
	• Focus on RELATIONSHIP

Exercise: How can we adapt our sales process to be more effective with I styles?

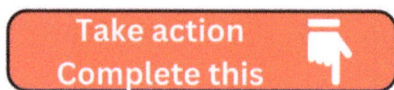

Take action
Complete this

Ways that we can improve our sales process to I styles are:

Recognising a S style

Recognising an S style:	
 ORATION SUPPORT ILITY	• Agreeable, welcoming manner – easy-going • Softer way of speaking, less forceful in groups • Moderate, methodical pace • Attentive, patient listener • Calm, gentle demeanour • Displays of modesty and accommodating others • Reluctance to commit quickly – wants to take their time • Reflective – can overthink things and be reluctant to change • Caution or hesitancy in making decisions • Prefers being in the background as a supporter • Likes others being in control and making decisions • Genuine, supportive, caring • Systems-oriented and will follow a clear process • Unassertive or uncritical – likes to please

	• Slow to open up but very loyal and supportive when connected • Avoids confrontation and can be quite sensitive when others don't consider their feelings
What S styles want in a buying experience	• Reliability – they want to know they can trust you • Sincerity and a genuine approach • Thoughtfulness and personal connection • Know them as an individual and care about them – not just the sale • Dependability and knowing that you'll be there to help them throughout • Reassurance that this is the right decision for them • Testimonials or stories about how other people have achieved outcomes • A friendly relationship with empathy for their situation
Pitching to an S	• Be patient, build trust, slow down, be willing to listen • Draw out their opinions • Explore their doubts and address their concerns • Connect with them on a personal level – don't make it all about business

	• Show them step-by-step what the process looks like
	• Provide solid evidence of reliability (testimonials, case studies, stories, guarantees, after-sale support)
	• Make them feel safe and supported to buy
	• Focus on RELIABILITY

Exercise: How can we adapt our sales process to be more effective with S styles?

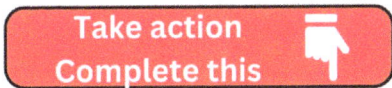

Take action
Complete this

Ways that we can improve our sales process to S styles are:

Recognising a C style

Recognising a C style:	• Questioning, sceptical
CHAL **C** ACCURACY STAE	• Cautious, reserved, reflective
	• Analytical, systematic
	• Carefully consider their options and risks
	• Unlikely to display great enthusiasm or animation – even if they like what they see
	• Little use for small talk and steers the discussion away from personal territory

	• Task-oriented
	• Uncomfortable being put on the spot
	• Bases decisions on objective information rather than emotion
	• Black and white in approach – it's either right or it isn't
	• Focused on quality and getting it right – even if it takes a little longer
	• Identifies risks that other people may not see and asks challenging questions
What C styles want in a buying experience	• High-quality products and services
	• Evidence to evaluate the effectiveness of your solution
	• Confidence in the merit of your offer
	• Details and depth of analysis that links to outcomes
	• No surprises – they want to depend on you and ensure there are no hidden problems down the line
	• Competency and expertise – know your business and be good at what you do
	• Support your claims with evidence and details
	• Talk through the concept logically and analytically with facts and data
Pitching to a C	• Prove your expertise by referring to your track record

- Provide the logic, facts, and reasoning behind your recommendations

- Give them space to reflect, analyse, and ask questions

- Prepare them in advance for the information required – don't put them on the spot

- Allow them to be right in their thinking – disagree with the facts, not the person

- Keep on task, and don't get distracted or sidetracked

- Use an agenda

- Provide the details

- Support them to understand the process and thinking behind your solution

- Focus on REASONING

Exercise: How can we adapt our sales process to be more effective with C styles?

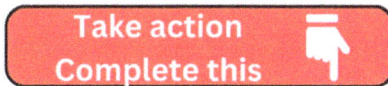

**Take action
Complete this**

Ways that we can improve our sales process to C styles are:

"Make it simple but significant. It needs to be easy, relevant, and important."

– Naomi Oyston

SALES & SERVICE RESOURCES

What is it?

Your Sales Playbook should include a simple and easy reference guide for common resources to support your sales activities with hyperlinks in place for each document and file. You may like to consider an intranet or database to ensure that everyone has access to the most current version.

If content is highly relevant to a sales conversation and easy to access, your people are more likely to use it.

To ensure your content is relevant and easy to find you should consider:

1. **Categories:** What are the logical topics that your salespeople would need in simple terms?

   Examples – competitor information, objection handling, trade shows and events, industry intelligence, sales collateral, customer communications, branding and images

2. **Tags:** Within each category you may like to set up tags according to themes.

   Example – under "objection handling", a tag could be "pricing"; or under "competitor information", a tag could be a specific competitor

3. **Searchability:** Firstly, ensure your salespeople are aware of the resources and that the content is easily

and quickly at their fingertips, through keyword search if possible.

4. **Updated regularly:** Ideally, all team members should be able to quickly upload information into the resources; however, this also means that someone will need to be responsible for periodic audits to ensure the content remains accurate and relevant.

Why does it matter?

Your Sales Playbook is a living, breathing document that will grow with use and ideally require regular updates. This process ensures that everyone is using the current version of materials and everyone is singing off the same hymn sheet. Your people should be regularly contributing to the resources section and sharing information from their day-to-day roles.

Exercise: What Resources should be referenced in our Sales Playbook?

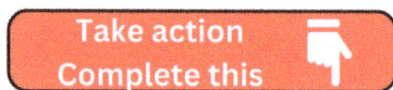

**Take action
Complete this**

Some examples of resources to consider include:

- Software systems user guides

- Email templates

- Style guide and branding pack

- Job descriptions and KPIs

- Best question guide

- Pricing authorities

- Case studies and success stories

- Scripting for calls and appointment setting

- LinkedIn profile requirements; company page support

- Competitor analysis

- Marketing programs in place

Putting it into Action: In summary

1. To know and to not do is to not know. When we've defined best practices across each of the key sales areas, we need to put it into action.

2. Results = Quantity of activity x Quality of activity x Consistency of activity. To achieve more successful outcomes, we need to improve one (or more) of these areas.

3. 80% of our results are created through 20% of our activities – these are called high payoff activities and it's essential to get these right.

4. No matter what business we are in, we are all in the people business. Our interpersonal skills and ability to

build relationships and engage with others is essential for our success.

5. There are certain principles of influence that, when used effectively, can increase the likelihood of compliance (YES) and reduce the likelihood of resistance (NO) to our suggestions.

6. There are four different personality types as defined within the DISC Personality Profiling framework. We could have all of these in the same room and each requires a different approach to engage and influence. We need to be aware of our own personal styles and how to identify the styles of others styles as well as adapting to their needs.

7. A Resources or Reference Section should be included in the Sales Playbook as a go-to place for additional sales and service materials.

"Now this is not the end. It is not even the beginning. But it is perhaps, the end of the beginning."

– Winston Churchill

CONCLUSION & NEXT STEPS

Congratulations!

You've reached this far, and by now, you'll have a good understanding of WHAT should be included in your Sales Playbook, WHY it matters, WHO needs to be involved, and HOW much VALUE you can create for your people, organisation, and customers through adapting a Best Practice Sales & Service Excellence approach.

You will also be able to see how your Sales Playbook can create the structure for quality, consistency, predictability, and continuous improvement across all Sales and Service aspects of your business.

By following this system, you will set your people up for success, scale your business, and delight your customers through working smarter, not harder.

The truth, however, is that just knowing all of this alone will not transform anything until it is put into action. They say knowledge is power, but I believe knowledge applied is power. Until then, knowledge is about as useful as an ash tray on a motorbike or a chocolate teapot – while they're nice to have, they don't really help you much.

To know and to not do is to not know...

The next step is to tailor this playbook to your unique business needs and build your own Sales Playbook, as this is where the rubber hits the road and you begin creating powerful transformation for your business.

SALES PLAYBOOK TEMPLATE

Prepared for:

YOU

SHiNE
executive

CLARITY TO SEE. CAPABILITY TO ACHIEVE. CONFIDENCE TO SHINE.

If you haven't already done so, here's how you can download your FREE Sales Playbook template (Word format) so that you can get started now:

www.shineexecutive.com.au/playbooktemplate

Download Now

You will no doubt see how important this is for your business. I'm sure that, like most business leaders, you'd like this to be in place as a priority. I can put my hand on my heart and promise you that it works when you do the work!

The concepts within this Sales Playbook are very simple – but this does not always mean it is easy to create, especially when you are juggling multiple priorities already.

From here on out, you have three clear choices:

1. *Do nothing at all:* I hope you've enjoyed the read and I'm sorry you won't get to enjoy the benefits, but thanks for hanging out with me along the way!

2. *Create a solid action plan:* refer to our section on Preparing to Create Your Playbook as a guide and get moving, beginning with your strong WHY.

3. *Fast track this process:* leverage the knowledge of experts to create a powerful and effective best practice resource as quickly and efficiently as possible

by working with us. To explore further, visit: www. shineexecutive.com.au/playbook-workwithus

Whatever choice you make, I truly wish you every success in your business and very much appreciate your interest in this topic. My strongest hope is that I've created a Raving Fan of Sales Playbooks and that you'll be delighted with the results of having invested in this process.

In the meantime, please don't be a stranger – let's connect on LinkedIn or feel free to drop me an email to: naomi@ shineexecutive.com.au

I'd love to hear from you!

WE'D LOVE TO HELP

Helping people like you is what we do day in, day out, and we love what we do.

We have over 20 years of experience in helping others to grow, learn, achieve, and shine through building clarity, capability, and confidence. We specialise in creating high performing teams through training workshops, consulting, coaching, leadership development, interpersonal or relationship skills, EQ, and skill building programs.

Our passion is your success!

We have worked across multiple industries and we know the key success drivers of business. We understand the sales and service processes but, most importantly, we also understand people! We are here to help create the most positive, engaging, and powerful Sales Playbook strategy by working with you and your team to unpack their knowledge, experience, insights, and combine this with best practice processes to create the right formula that meets your unique business needs and culture.

From here, leverage is the next logical step.

What is leverage? In business, leverage is the act of achieving more with less effort, which is the first level of scaling your business.

It's a combination of mindset, toolkit, strategy, support, and accountability.

When this is done right, you can look forward to enjoying a leveraged sales team where your systems, processes, and culture supports collective success. This begins with defining and then building better Sales & Service habits to create the high-value activities which drive the results that matter.

Is this program right for you?

Perhaps. Let's see.

The principles in this Sales Playbook have been drawn from over 20 years of work within high performance sales and service environments, combined with "standing on the shoulders of greatness" by discovering global best practices from the world's leading sales and performance workplace culture experts.

We have done the work and know how to provide solutions to the frustrations you're feeling and experiencing now.

Just as it's difficult to give yourself a good haircut, it can be hard to see your own blind spots, challenges, and opportunities, especially when there is a high level of unconscious competence where you don't consciously know what you know – you just do it.

Some of our other clients tell us that they love having us on their team to provide valuable insights, which keep them focused and engaged. We help our clients to keep things moving while also reducing the overwhelm that inevitably pops up from time to time.

You're not alone. We would love to be on your team if this is the right solution for you.

The next step is simple – it all starts with a conversation to see if we're a good fit – or not.

Follow the link below so we can schedule some time to discuss.

www.shineexecutive.com.au/playbook-workwithus

ABOUT THE AUTHOR

Naomi Oyston has more than twenty years of leadership experience within the corporate, financial, and SME business sectors.

She has had extensive executive level success, with direct responsibility for leading the implementation and performance assessment of Customer Service Excellence, Sales Performance, Productivity & Leadership training within Commonwealth Bank Business Banking. She has also led the Leadership Performance Coaching Team at Suncorp, with responsibility for Branch, Financial Planning, Home Lending, and Business Banking Leadership Development. Within Heritage Bank, she has designed and delivered a group-wide Sales Through Service program along with playing an integral role in developing a contemporary customer conversation framework and has also delivered a Risk Management program for leaders.

As an independent consultant, she has worked across multiple industries including government, corporate, financial, insurance, mining, manufacturing, trade services, aged care, consulting, retail, technology, pharmaceutical, and education to help leaders to drive exceptional people to achieve high performance outcomes.

Naomi specialises in providing bespoke solutions that meet the unique needs of her clients by gaining a deep understanding of each client's needs, challenges, and opportunities. Prior to setting up her consultancy, she operated her own successful commercial finance broking business and knows firsthand the challenges of creating a sustainable, profitable operation based on strong business-to-business relationships.

Naomi judged on the Telstra Business Women's Awards, the AIM Leadership Excellence Awards and is recognised by the Who's Who of Australian Women for her contribution to mentoring women in the financial and business sectors.

Naomi is passionate about helping her clients to focus on results that matter. She creates continuous, incremental improvement through combining street proven systems and processes with exemplary people skills and a culture of sustainability, using a head, heart, and soul approach to success.

Qualifications

- Certificate IV Training & Assessment (TAE40122)
- Diploma of Positive Psychology
- Diploma of Business (Management)
- DISC Facilitator
- Five Behaviours of a Cohesive Team Facilitator
- NLP Master Practitioner
- Jack Daly Sales Leadership Facilitator
- Cohen Brown & Sales ITV Trainer
- Master Workplace Coaching Trainer
- QO2 - Opportunities Obstacles Facilitator
- Professional Speakers Australia – Professional Member

TESTIMONIALS

Suncorp Bank – GROWTH Coaching for Leaders

"Naomi was fantastic, provided real world examples and relevancy. I feel like the session was very valuable and helped me to structure how I can best coach my people." Stephanie Colina

"Great session. I was nervous about the role plays but it was a great success and I'm much more confident now". Frances McAulay.

"The program was excellent, well thought out and designed." Veena Kini

"Thank you for a wonderful day of learning. I've taken away a lot and will use the skills today with my people." Loralie Evans

"Short, sharp but to the point. Exactly what we need for this space." Melody Wang

Bank of South Pacific – Building Better Sales Habits

Naomi delivered Sales & Service Excellence training throughout multiple departments of BSP with excellent feedback and engagement. She was able to bring out the best in others by making learning fun with high levels of interaction, reflection and self discovery while sharing

practical examples that were simple and relatable within our unique cultural environment. Participants left the training feeling energised, confident and equipped for success. Andy Roberts

Was an awesome training experience. Naomi had practical examples for each of the concepts taught. Regardless of participants not having sales backgrounds and being in different business roles, the concepts taught are relevant in our everyday roles. Janet Seta

The overall training experience has been an awakening moment. I am now more aware of my role as a salesperson. Nepthalai Aukiri

Heritage Bank – Building Better Sales Habits

Naomi was knowledgeable with real hands-on experience. She is engaging and makes sense. A great opportunity to reflect on current skills, share the best practice and plan to move forward. Deb Parker

Naomi created real value and set up skills that have endless opportunities. Naomi is very engaging. Two great days where I took away so much valuable information. Jennifer Rowley

Lovely fresh, depth, good balance. Core material very well suited to audience. Made things clear and put into words what comes natural. Naomi had fun and was the right balance between relaxed and professional. Core material very well suited to audience. Terri Morris

Excellent. Very credible as Naomi has past experience as a lender/leader/coach. Great rapport building with the class. I loved the content and found the course to be very beneficial to our current roles. Michelle Kuskie

Estia Health – Managing Conflict

"I loved the session and how it was presented. Excellent." Michelle McGregor

"Naomi was very good at facilitating input from participants in the group & it made me feel supported and part of one family." Robert Johnson

"Very engaging, interactive, approachable and enjoyable session." Donna Morley

Aurizon – Managing Conflict & Difficult Customers

"Naomi is a fantastic facilitator, very relatable and confident in her knowledge" Tamika Scriven

"Excellent facilitator, Naomi was open and related it to her life which made us comfortable in sharing." Emma Lamke

"Naomi is a wonderful facilitator - she was open, honest and optimistic. She used real life examples that were relatable in practice." Mariah Smith

"I feel everyone would benefit from this program, whether it's in the workplace or home." Sue Midford

"Absolutely loved the day - Naomi was spectacular" Alindi Neaton

Abacus dx - Leadership Development

"An excellent program with so much great content. Naomi is a fantastic facilitator - her experience is priceless and her approach created such a great learning and sharing environment." Chiara Campo

"Naomi is an amazing facilitator and her approach is very effective. The program is vast but covered extremely well and greatly appreciated." Natasha Fuller

"Naomi was fantastic - she varied her tone and the program content to suit us which was just perfect." Christine Johnson

Henley / Plantation Homes - Leadership Development

"Great training and great knowledge! Naomi is an amazing facilitator and very helpful." Florence Soemhro

"Naomi is the best instructor I have ever had." Joel Sawatzky

Master Electricians Australia – Quality Member Engagement

"Fantastic – Naomi – you are so relevant and down to earth – truly refreshing. You are very relatable and friendly.. Great to gather other people's opinions and thoughts – always learn more that way. A great learning activity." Debbie Lucas

"Naomi was great. In a short period, she was able to discern our needs, work with 3 senior managers across different functional groups and designed a session that was engaging, full of ideas and learnings that shared our collective strengths to combat our perceived weakness. It was a really productive and enjoyable day – we achieved everything we needed and more." Jason O'Dwyer

ACKNOWLEDGEMENTS

I've heard it takes a village to raise a child...

It also takes a village to produce a book like this one. The book has been created through a combination of standing on the shoulders of greatness, learning with a ferocious curiosity, having amazing relationships with colleagues who have become friends, and embracing the resilience required to step up, fall down, and then step back up again and again throughout the inevitable highs and lows of a 30-year sales career to define what works – and what doesn't.

I truly believe that we learn more from our failures than from our successes and that humility along the way to mastery is character-building. True confidence comes from overcoming failure and finding strength in yourself to deal with things you never realised you could.

On a personal note, I am incredibly grateful for the people who are closest to me. My husband, Andy, for his tireless support; my daughter, Tiana, for giving me a reason to be the best role model I can be; and my beautiful circle of friends whom I appreciate and value so much.

Professionally, I have been incredibly blessed throughout my career, especially in the banking and finance sector. Back in the early 1990s (in the days of affirmative action) while working for Westpac Bank, I was identified as a high potential woman and given the invaluable gift of a fast-track leadership mentoring program called Springboard

Women's Development. This program was a turning point for me as it helped me to believe that much more was possible than I had always thought, and that I could achieve my wildest dreams if I worked hard enough.

The program gave me rewards on so many levels personally, professionally, and financially, but most of all, it gave me a ferocious desire to learn, grow, and achieve. Because of the gift I received through this, I wanted to pay it forward and help others to also achieve. So my love of learning, growing, and helping others to succeed was born.

Working in banking, especially in the commercial sector, helped me to quickly understand the success drivers of businesses and the unique challenges that business owners face every day in keeping their doors open. I was fortunate to work with some amazing leaders who taught me what great looked like, along with some others who taught me what not-so-great looks like – we learn just as much from both. The foundations that I gained through the commercial banking sector allowed me to adapt to almost any business environment and to see the commonalities that are across all industries.

I've met many masters along the way who have impacted my journey. Some of these people are teachers, some are friends or colleagues, and many are clients. I'm grateful for all of them, especially my clients who have taught me as much as I've taught them. I feel blessed to have had the opportunities to serve you.

Lastly, a big thank you to everyone involved in bringing this book together and ensuring it is in the hands of those who can benefit most from it. There are many special people (too many to mention individually) who have played an important role in this project and I am very grateful for your support, expertise, and professionalism.

And finally, to you, the reader. Thank you for choosing my book and taking the time to broaden your perspective on creating a comprehensive sales strategy. I wish you every success in your business and in all areas of your life.

And please remember – **We are all meant to Shine!**

Our Deepest Fear

Our deepest fear is not that we are inadequate.

Our deepest fear is that we are powerful beyond measure.

It is our light, not our darkness that most frightens us. We ask ourselves, "Who am I to be brilliant, gorgeous, talented, fabulous?" Actually, who are you not to be? You are a child of God. Your playing small does not serve the world. There is nothing enlightened about shrinking so that other people won't feel insecure around you.

We are all meant to shine, as children do. We were born to make manifest the glory that is within us.

It is not just in some of us, it's in everyone. And as we let our own light shine, we unconsciously give other people permission to do the same.

As we are liberated from our own fear, our presence automatically liberates others.

— Marianne Williamson

A Return to Love: Reflections on the Principles of "A Course in Miracles"

www.ingramcontent.com/pod-product-compliance
Lightning Source LLC
Chambersburg PA
CBHW040920210326
41597CB00030B/5143